Heilman
2067 Golf Drive
Culpeper, VA 22701

JOSEPH
OF
ARIMATHEA

JOSEPH

OF

ARIMATHEA

THE EXTRAORDINARY CALLING OF ORDINARY PEOPLE

KEN COSTA

iDisciple Publishing
2555 Northwinds Parkway
Alpharetta GA 30009, USA

www.thefeddagency.com

Published in association with The Fedd Agency, Inc., a literary agency.

ISBN: 978-1-949784-31-2
eISBN: 978-1-949784-32-9

Printed in China

First Edition 15 14 13 12 11 / 10 9 8 7 6 5 4 3 2

TABLE OF CONTENTS

"AFTER THESE THINGS JOSEPH OF ARIMATHEA, WHO WAS A DISCIPLE OF JESUS, BUT SECRETLY FOR FEAR OF THE JEWS, ASKED PILATE THAT HE MIGHT TAKE AWAY THE BODY OF JESUS, AND PILATE GAVE HIM PERMISSION. SO HE CAME AND TOOK AWAY HIS BODY. NICODEMUS ALSO, WHO EARLIER HAD COME TO JESUS BY NIGHT, CAME BRINGING A MIXTURE OF MYRRH AND ALOES, ABOUT SEVENTY-FIVE POUNDS IN WEIGHT. SO THEY TOOK THE BODY OF JESUS AND BOUND IT IN LINEN CLOTHS WITH THE SPICES, AS IS THE BURIAL CUSTOM OF THE JEWS. NOW IN THE PLACE WHERE HE WAS CRUCIFIED THERE WAS A GARDEN, AND IN THE GARDEN A NEW TOMB IN WHICH NO ONE HAD YET BEEN LAID. SO BECAUSE OF THE JEWISH DAY OF PREPARATION, SINCE THE TOMB WAS CLOSE AT HAND, THEY LAID JESUS THERE."

FOREWORD

JENTEZEN FRANKLIN

As Christians, we all play a role in the redemption story. We get to be a part of the Kingdom of God coming to earth. In the mundanity of everyday life, we tend to forget this truth, but the everyday is often where our lights shine the brightest. World-changers are built in the ordinary. No matter where we find ourselves, in every aspect of our lives, we can worship God through our character and excellence.

In *Joseph of Arimathea*, Ken Costa, a theologian and successful businessman, provides an interesting character study of Joseph of Arimathea, a businessman and secret disciple of Jesus. During Jesus' life, Joseph followed Jesus surreptitiously as he was afraid associating with Jesus would destroy his career. After Jesus' death, something shifted in Joseph—he bravely identified with Jesus and used his clout and resources within the community to give Jesus an honorable burial. It took courage to associate with someone who was killed for being a revolutionary, but Joseph took the risk because he believed Jesus was who He said He was. In Joseph's search for truth, He found it in Jesus.

Ken, much like Joseph, is a man who seeks Truth and is willing to follow Jesus no matter the cost. Ken displays through the story of Joseph, as well as stories of his own life, that the world isn't divided by sacred and secular. Rather, we can worship Jesus in whatever role we have on this earth—whether that's as a pastor, a businessman, a student, a teacher, etc. No one calling is higher than the next. As long as we are obedient to God and generous with our gifts and resources, we are being faithful disciples and stewards.

Throughout Ken's life, he has wrestled with finding his place amidst the injustice in the world and with how to be a disciple in a secular world. From growing up in South Africa during apartheid to deciding whether to become an ordained minister or stay in banking, Ken has navigated difficult challenges, all the while relying on God and seeking to do what is right—no matter how hard it might be. Ken has been a voice of truth and reason in every role he's found himself in. People look up to him and value his insight because he is a man of character; he is someone who finds opportunity to worship and honor God in the mundane moments of everyday life. Character is built overtime in the everyday, and world-changers are people of character. Ken and Joseph both took the road less traveled in pivotal moments in history and their faithfulness and devotion has left a significant impact on the world.

In *Joseph of Arimathea*, Ken reimagines the story of Jesus' death and resurrection from a perspective that is far different from the perspectives we often hear. Ken's thoughtful and wise words shine a light on people of the small print—those who do behind-the-scenes work faithfully because they desire to honor God's faithfulness to them. In these insightful and relatable descriptions of Joseph, Ken shows us that people of the small print have an important role in the story of Jesus and they have an important place in the Kingdom.

Joseph's obedience and devotion led him to be a key part of the resurrection story—the greatest and most meaningful story of all time. His character and courage led him to the opportunity to be a part of this incredible and world-changing moment in time. Being a disciple is not about the fame or praise; being a follower of Jesus should never be about that. It's about the honor of getting to be part of the redemption story. It's about a person who lifts up the One who is worthy of praise—just as Joseph did. Just as Ken does.

This book is for anyone who has felt unsure of their place in the Kingdom. Anyone discouraged by the mundanity of everyday life. For anyone who has doubted or questioned their calling. For anyone who relates to the identifier of secret disciple. We all, like Joseph and Ken, have opportunities in our daily lives to remember the role that we play in the redemption story: to seek truth and act boldly in light of what we find.

PREFACE

Working as an investment banker in London is a never-ending ride of ups and downs. Long hours and flexible travel schedules make you a permanent passenger with no certainty where or when the day will end. With the responsibilities of providing financial forecasts, leading diverse teams, and analyzing data, the high-stress environment takes its toll.

One evening twenty years ago, after a long week and deep contemplation about whether or not I was in the right line of work, I left my office earlier than usual to hear one of the leading prophetic voices in America speaking at one of the largest conference centers in London. I must confess, I was dipping in and out of his message. The challenges and complexities of the day's events were still hovering in the shadows of my mind as I tried to focus on the sermon, when I suddenly heard my name.

"Ken."

As I squinted into the spotlight that shone directly in front of me, I realized I was being called out. I rose up from my seat, shocked that a man I had never met before was calling out my name from the stage in front of thousands of people.

He cleared his voice, looked directly at me, and said something that resonated with me profoundly and emboldened me to stay in finance and to be a witness in my workplace. But then he added an after-thought, a kind of postscript, that has stuck with me for more than two decades:

"Ken, the Lord has brought you to a place where, like Joseph of Arimathea, you are going to be used to present the Lord's resurrected body to those around you, so take heart from that."

I must admit in the moment it meant very little. I wrote the word down, nodded, and smiled politely. In fact, his comments suggesting I resembled Joseph of Arimathea remained for decades a forgotten, random addendum.

Joseph of Arimathea appears in the small print of the biblical narrative: a footnote, a postscript to the great salvation story. I knew about Old Testament Joseph, the prime minister of Egypt. I had often studied the highs and lows of his life's journey and tried to apply his life lessons to my own life. And Joseph, the husband of Mary, came to mind at least annually at Christmas. But Joseph of Arimathea? With the exception of a few verses in each Gospel, Joseph disappears off the pages of Scripture just as quickly as he arrives. He was merely a bit player in the dramatic story of Good Friday and almost seems dispensable to the biblical narrative. Who was this man who was mentioned in only sixteen verses, in all four of the Gospels? And why should I identify with him? How could this minor character speak into my life?

Little did I know that two decades later, when writing *Strange Kingdom: Meditations on the Cross*, the Joseph of Arimathea comment would finally make sense. While doing research for *Strange Kingdom*, a passage from Luke's Gospel leapt out at me:

> *Now there was a man named Joseph, from the Jewish town of Arimathea. He was a member of the council, a good and righteous man, who had not consented to their decision and action; and he was looking for the kingdom of God.*
> - Luke 23:50-51

Joseph had not consented to the council's decision and action regarding the death of Jesus. In other words, *Joseph was not part of the majority*.

I was gripped. *Not part of the majority* was now on a continuing loop in my mind. The phrase simply would not go away.

A perfectly average man, standing up against the majority of religious leaders who wanted to see an innocent man crucified. Joseph, a businessman, a person of the small print who rose to the occasion. Sixteen lines—that's all he was given. As a businessman myself, I began to become absorbed with Joseph,

> JOSEPH HAD NOT CONSENTED TO THE COUNCIL'S DECISION AND ACTION REGARDING THE DEATH OF JESUS. IN OTHER WORDS, JOSEPH WAS NOT PART OF THE MAJORITY.

who, in so many ways, described many features of my own life and fascinated me with the mysterious nature of his biblical cameo. It is this fascination with Joseph of Arimathea, who, through the millennia, could still speak into my life and many others lives, that led me to write this book.

So, what do we know about this average Joe? Well, we know nothing about Joseph's early life or upbringing. Arimathea, the place where he was raised, is not mentioned again in the Bible nor do we know precisely where it is—a place just as ambiguous as the man Scripture attests came from there.

We *do* know that Joseph was a member of the Jewish Sanhedrin (an assembly of seventy-one rabbis appointed to council). Considering that to be a member of the council meant you were in a position of prominence, we can safely assume he was a wealthy person of influence. We know from the story of Jesus throwing the merchants out of the temple that the temple tax was a source of great revenue that Joseph most likely benefited from.

Joseph was a secret disciple of Jesus. He probably did not want to come out as a public supporter of Jesus since many in the council believed Jesus to be a heretic. All Jewish leaders of that time were expecting the Messiah, but Jesus did not meet their expectations of a Messiah. Most people weren't expecting the Messiah to be born in a manger. They weren't expecting the savior of the world to be a carpenter's son. The majority did not imagine that the long-awaited Messiah would be stripped, beaten, spat upon with degradation, and crucified.

But Joseph *was not part of the majority.*

I believe when Joseph saw this innocent man dying on the cross, something changed in him. In that moment, this Jewish man saw the Messiah for whom he desperately longed. Others might have seen the crucified Jesus as a failed miracle worker and leader. Yet when Joseph saw the crucified Christ, his faith came alive.

Mark tells us that Joseph went boldly to Pilate to ask for the body. Joseph saw this as an opportunity to honor the man who he silently followed; Joseph took this moment to declare his devotion publicly. Associating with a criminal would surely tarnish his reputation, but he stepped forward anyway. He knew he had the means to bury Jesus properly.

Surely you would expect the body of Jesus to be given to his family or at least to the disciples, as was common practice? Despite being trained and prepared for three years for this moment, Jesus' disciples had fled. There was no sign of Peter. Only hours before, he had denied the very one he promised never to disown only hours before. John, the beloved disciple, had disappeared. The others had scattered or watched "from a distance" with the women as Jesus' body hung hopelessly on a cross (Luke 23:49). Jesus was just another corpse soon to be thrown on the mounting pile of bodies. Just another crucifixion. Just another failed prophet. Where were his "devoted" followers at such a crucial time? Joseph of Arimathea saw this as his opportunity to step forward.

Pilate gave Joseph the body of this executed criminal to be washed and buried in accordance with Jewish Law. Joseph performed these rituals with another secret disciple, Nicodemus.

Nicodemus, a fellow member of the council, bought spices

of unimaginable cost in order to embalm the body. Both he and Joseph fully knew the embalming would make them ritually impure at the start of the Passover feast. They sacrificed their cleanliness, money, time, and reputations in order to pay respect to a man who had changed their lives. They took the body, wrapped it in cloths made of linen with the spices that the ritual required, and laid Jesus in the tomb. Because of their prominence, they would have had enough dignitaries, servants, and people under their authority to whom they could have delegated the task, but they bloodied and contaminated themselves in order to show honor to an apparently failed Messiah.

I doubt that either of them knew that Jesus would rise from the dead, and yet they carried the weight of the savior in their hands—the unique privilege all theirs.

Joseph and Nicodemus were not the leading disciples. They were not leaders anointed to take on the movement. They were silent disciples. Secret disciples. Nicodemus had come to Jesus "by night" under the cover of darkness so no one could see (John 3). Jesus revealed himself as the savior of the world to Nicodemus. Joseph had watched Jesus from a distance, learning about him and growing in faith. We read in the Gospel of John that one of the reasons why people were scared of coming out as disciples of Jesus was because they were intimidated by the religious leaders:

> I DOUBT THAT EITHER OF THEM KNEW THAT JESUS WOULD RISE FROM THE DEAD, AND YET THEY CARRIED THE WEIGHT OF THE SAVIOR IN THEIR HANDS—THE UNIQUE PRIVILEGE ALL THEIRS.

"the Jews had already agreed that if anyone should confess Jesus to be Christ, he was to be put out of the synagogue" (John 9:22). Though Joseph was afraid to profess his allegiance to Jesus while he was alive, in the face of Jesus' death, he stepped up.

Joseph knew this was the price of admitting to being a follower of Jesus. How extraordinary that he would do this publicly *after* Jesus was dead. He had nothing to gain and so much to lose. Yet even in Christ's death, Joseph was willing to identify himself and risk excommunication by being associated with Jesus. Despite the fear he had, Joseph overcame his reticence, even amidst the crowd baying at Jesus.

Again and again, I keep coming back to phrase:

He was not part of the majority.
He was not part of the majority.
He was not part of the majority.

Fast-forward many centuries, and that same fear of being ostracized and rejected due to a public belief in Christ exists today. As a Christian businessman, I relate deeply to Nicodemus and to Joseph of Arimathea. Like many of you reading this book, I know the sense of being a secret disciple at work.

Often Christians feel that we are dismissed in a culture which demonizes our values and beliefs. So much so that we fear speaking up against a prevailing ethos of materialism, consumerism, and fluid morality, which changes to our whims to make room for individualistic desires. But we can learn from Joseph about the vital nature of speaking up and of not being part of the majority, even when it appears that we will be drowned out by the power of others' voices and the apparent intellectual superiority of those arguing against us. I cannot remember a time when moral dilemmas were so complex and widespread as they are now. These days it seems that unity, reconciliation, and repair are beyond our grasp. Populist rhetoric, fueled by enraged social media commentators, has shaped the global body. Justice has to be fought for every day on issues we thought had long since been settled. And freedom of speech, the hallmark of our educational institutions, is constantly under attack.

So, how do we as Christians respond to this uncertain, angst-ridden world? How do we find the courage to stand up for justice? To stand firm when a prevailing majority opinion, which is unfair and unjust, threatens to take hold of our society? These are questions I struggle with every day.

Growing up in apartheid South Africa, when the prevailing ethos was that black people were inherently deficient and needed to live separately from white people, I wrestled with these questions from a young age. I attended an all-white school, used all-white public bathrooms, and attended an all-white church. All the while, there was a burning sense of injustice. I did not want to be part of this worldview. How could I use my privilege and resources to fight for justice?

I clearly remember when the architect of apartheid and prime minister at the time, Dr. Verwoerd, was assassinated in Parliament. As prefect of my school, I was asked to speak at the memorial service which our school was required to have to honor

Dr. Verwoerd. The headmaster asked what I would speak on, and I told him that the theme would be "He that lives by the sword will perish by the sword," addressing the hideous consequences of racial segregation. I was immediately removed from my position for being a rebellious student and was then severely reprimanded for my lack of compassion and compliance. I was only sixteen, hotheaded but passionate about justice, and I felt at that moment that I wanted to stand against the prevailing white majority's view supporting racial segregation. So I did.

From then on, I publicly worked against the will of the authorities, believing that academic freedom and the right of all people to attend a university without regard to race, sex, or religion was paramount. Despite incurring long-lasting wrath from authorities, I knew it was the right thing to do, even if it was just a footnote in the liberation history of South Africa. I accepted this as a minor, unrecognized part in the struggle for freedom and justice that I longed for all people to have. This burning sense of injustice gave me the courage, which I did not normally have, to be able to withstand the oppression of the police state.

In the early seventies, I left South Africa and came to study in England at the University of Cambridge, where faith came alive and I joined a group of committed Christians. I was not part of the university majority whose ethos was deeply secular and opposed to any form of religious experience. Being a Christian at university meant that I had to swim against the defining secular tide of society and academia. I wished to test the foundations of my faith to see whether it was but a temporary whim, and I decided to enroll as a student in the theology department. It was the high tide of doubt, and few lecturers believed in the inspiration of Scripture. Swimming against this liberal tide was a minority activity.

After university, I joined the greatest financial center in the world, The City of London, where I am still active after more than forty years. Being a Christian in the workplace is incredibly difficult. But I believe that my workstation is also my worship station. I empathize with Joseph of Arimathea who kept his faith quiet for fear of the Jews. I certainly kept my faith quiet in my workplace for a long time. All the while, I was thinking, *What would my colleagues think? Will I be promoted if I am not ambitious and cutthroat? If I am not money-driven or as brazen as the rest of the financial industry, will I be respected?*

> THIS IS THE GREAT CHALLENGE FOR ANYONE IN THE WORKPLACE: FACING DIFFICULT DECISIONS AND STRESS WITH THE ADDED UNCERTAINTY OF HOW TO INCORPORATE YOUR FAITH INTO YOUR WORK LIFE.

When I look at Joseph of Arimathea, I see a man who did the right thing amidst a whirlwind of anxiety and doubt filling his mind. As he looked towards the cross, he no doubt pondered what effect his decision to step forward would have on his everyday working relationships—his family, the council, his colleagues. This is the great challenge for anyone in the workplace: facing difficult decisions and stress with the added uncertainty of how to incorporate your faith into your work life.

Joseph captures the inner struggle of choosing what is right versus choosing what is convenient. He teaches us how to work through the moral complexities and dilemmas which we face each day in the workplace. He shows us how to channel our passion for justice with practical and pragmatic actions that impact the world through working with others. His example encourages us to stand up for and speak out on behalf of those who are voiceless—the marginalized and the rejected members of our society.

Joseph is a person who reaches through the verses of Scripture to our own generation in a powerful, relevant, and compelling way. He teaches us that the ordinary matters. An ordinary person, living an ordinary daily life, doing the daily duties and routines, can be a conduit and instrument in the hands of God to be used for His purposes and for His kingdom.

For the people who don't make the front page news, Joseph's life speaks to you. Joseph of Arimathea speaks from the small print of the great gospel story with a message of empathy and standing up for truth. Because he obeyed, God ended up using him to play a small but significant part in his rescue plan for humankind. Because he had courage, Joseph of Arimathea's actions changed the world. Joseph of Arimathea is the good news for the people of the small print. He exemplifies the extraordinary calling of ordinary people.

> JOSEPH OF ARIMATHEA IS THE GOOD NEWS FOR THE PEOPLE OF THE SMALL PRINT. HE EXEMPLIFIES THE EXTRAORDINARY CALLING OF ORDINARY PEOPLE.

God still looks for the Josephs and the people of the small print today—ordinary men and women who believe that God is not finished with the world which he created. Ordinary people of the

> AT A TIME WHEN INFLUENCE, FOLLOWERS, AND CLOUT ARE THE ORDER OF THE DAY, JOSEPH REMINDS US THAT SMALL ACTS OF FAITHFULNESS CAN LEAD TO ASTOUNDING INFLUENCE AND IMPACT.

small print who serve an extraordinary, all-powerful God.

Will you serve like Joseph of Arimathea, even when you don't fully understand? Will you stand up against the injustices in our society, even when it feels like you are swimming against the cultural tide?

Through the obedience of one person who was willing to be a mere footnote—a snapshot in history—the stage was set for the first cries of new birth and re-creation to burst forth. Through one small act of courage, Joseph said, *Yes. Yes, I will follow You. Yes, I will pay the price. Yes, I will partner with others to extend Your Kingdom's cause. Yes, I will gladly write myself into the story of God, even as a footnote in history, knowing that, in eternity, my part will be displayed on a grand canvas, too important to be missed, and too significant to be ignored.*

And God responded:

Your sacrifice is worth it.
There is no price too high to pay.
You counted the cost, and you will reap the rewards of your faithfulness.

Joseph is a portal through which we see our generation and its cultural narrative unfolding. God paints his story with individuals like Joseph—a story that uses the ordinary to achieve the amazing.

And as we take time to reflect upon the pictures each Gospel writer has placed on their easel, we see how an almost bypassed figure in Scripture, a man who leaves the pages of Scripture no sooner than he arrives, is, I believe, a person for our generation.

At a time when influence, followers, and clout are the order of the day, Joseph reminds us that small acts of faithfulness can lead to astounding influence and impact. As God paints on the canvas of His creation, the ordinary people of the small print matter. As you read about Joseph of Arimathea, my prayer is that you would feel, as I have felt, God's presence and begin to see yourself in His masterpiece.

01

A WALK THROUGH THE GALLERY

Now there was a man named Joseph, from the
Jewish town of Arimathea . . .
- Luke 23:50

When I think of story told through portraiture, I think of Winston Churchill, the former British Prime Minister, during the dark days of the Second World War. Many have tried to capture something of this man, by camera or brush. Whether it was Churchill in conference with his allies, or looking grim-faced and determined; whether with his family in the country, or coming out of a black taxi as he gives the famous two-fingered "V for Victory" salute: each portrait paints Churchill in a completely different light. Every one provoking and unearthing a range of responses in the viewer. This is the skill of the portrait artist or photographer. Each work offers scope for the creativity and inspiration of the artist, but whether portrayed as a family man or man of war, all are recognizably Churchill.

Perhaps my favorite, and the most famous, photograph of Churchill was done by Yousuf Karsh. Karsh is widely regarded as one of the best portrait photographers of all time. He had been waiting to photograph Churchill after he spoke before the Canadian Parliament. He wanted to capture Churchill in all his fullness. He wanted to express as much of his life as possible in a single photograph. Karsh, therefore, set up his camera and lighting the night before. In his book, *Faces of Our Time*, Karsh recounts how Churchill's mood was sour from the moment he walked through the door. He directed Churchill to sit in a chair, describing the scene as follows: "He was in no mood for portraiture and two minutes were all that he would allow me as he passed from the House of Commons chamber to an anteroom. Two niggardly minutes in which I must try to put on film a man who had already written or inspired a library of books, baffled all his biographers, filled the world with his fame and me, on this occasion, with dread."[1]

Churchill had not been told that he would be photographed. Despite his qualms, he relented, then pulled out a cigar, lit it, and began puffing away. Karsh recalls how Churchill's cigar was ever-present: "I held out an ashtray, but he would not dispose of it. I went back to my camera and made sure that everything was all right technically. I waited; he continued to chomp vigorously at his cigar. I waited. Then I spotted him and, without premeditation, but ever so respectfully, I said, 'Forgive me, sir,' and plucked the cigar out of his mouth. By the time I got back to my camera, he looked so belligerent he could have devoured me. It was at that instant that I took the photograph."

By plucking the cigar from Churchill's mouth without permission, Karsh was able to elicit a fantastic pose and facial expression from the great leader and thereby capture an exceptional photo.

This photo captures merely one facet of Churchill's personality and character. To recognize Churchill more fully, we would need all the portraits from every artist that sought to represent him artistically. Only then could we put them together to get a fully rounded picture of the man.

It is the same when the Gospel writers tell us the story of Christ's crucifixion. One after the other, the four Gospel writers—Matthew, Mark, Luke, and John—steady their hands. Each artist, with considered, thought-out brush strokes, uses different colors to paint upon a canvas their perspective of what transpired on that fatal weekend.

Four portraits. One exhibition. And one figure standing at the center of all four canvases: Jesus. Surrounding Jesus in these portraits are disciples who were important figures in His life. What makes this gallery particularly remarkable is this somewhat obscure figure who appears in all portraits but about whom we know very little. What we *do* know is that he was significant to the story of the resurrection of Christ. That figure is Joseph of Arimathea.

Each Gospel writer draws out a different dimension of this

man named Joseph. As all great portrait artists do, each brush stroke finds and captures an entire hinterland and tells us more about this unassuming character. Matthew, Mark, Luke, and John each show a different angle and expression of who this lone figure was. We have a handful of verses to help us piece together what we see—a regular man written into the divine story.

We know from the Gospel writers that Joseph was a man of prominence and a business person. He encountered some of the most acute moral dilemmas we face in our age. He was well known in his field, holding a position of power and influence. He was a member of the Jewish ruling council. He had a passion for justice, he stood up against the crowd, and he was not part of the majority that condemned Jesus. This was a man with a conscience who proclaimed values that aligned with his practice.

Like so many of our generation, Joseph knew the value of strategic partnerships. He was a rich man who used his riches well. He stewarded his affluence and his influence. He was not a theologian. He was not a church leader. He was a secret disciple. Just as many of us fear the opinions of our colleagues, he too feared his Jewish contemporaries. He was a reluctant follower, hesitant to share his faith in the mixing pot that was the Roman empire. He had the same fears, worries, and anxieties we all feel and encounter in our everyday environments. Yet he shows us what an encounter with Jesus Christ can do to an individual

HE WAS NOT A THEOLOGIAN. HE WAS NOT A CHURCH LEADER. HE WAS A SECRET DISCIPLE.

life. Joseph was transformed into a disciple who risked it all. He approached Pilate asking permission for the dead body of Jesus. He paid a price to anoint Jesus' body. He partnered with his friend Nicodemus to prepare the body for burial. And he placed Jesus in his own tomb. It is this one event that writes him into the pages of scripture forever.

The description of this man doesn't have the flair of a Lazarus raised from the dead. Nor does it match the excitement of Jesus healing the sick or cleansing ten lepers. However, Joseph's depiction strikes a chord with the contemporary mindset of ordinary laypeople more than most by emphasizing justice and conscience, as well as the use of power.

In a world in which power often supersedes small efforts, it is refreshing to read about ordinary people doing extraordinary things in order to resolve the great moral issues of our time. It's not just the big guns or the religious establishment who have a major impact on faith; it's not just those at the top of governments or big organizations that can effect change, but those at every level who face acute moral dilemmas and still do the right thing. The athlete who refuses to take the drugs, the politician who doesn't take a bribe, the journalist who stands up against fake news, the citizen who is not swept along by moments of madness but stays cool when the mob surrounds them. It is the man who requests to carry the dead body of Jesus and does not expect to be recorded in the pages of scripture.

Joseph of Arimathea is an example for the practical businessperson going to work every day. He is for the leader who has to chair meetings, lead teams, share strategy, and face the moral dilemmas of the workplace. He is for the woman who seeks to balance the practical, the pragmatic, and the spiritual. He is for those who don't make the front page news. He speaks to our generation from the small print of the great gospel story with a message of devotion and discipleship.

> HE SPEAKS TO OUR GENERATION FROM THE SMALL PRINT OF THE GREAT GOSPEL WITH A MESSAGE OF DEVOTION AND DISCIPLESHIP.

In a world where harsh compromises have to be made every single day, we struggle with issues of confidence and conscience. How can we live with integrity and spiritual insight in our everyday lives? This is the great challenge of everyone today. Whether you are in the workplace, in a church, in a voluntary organization, you face hard and difficult decisions that affect the lives of others.

As we examine and move from canvas to canvas in the gallery, we view Joseph's life from a new angle, a fresh perspective; we see this remarkable man of the utmost relevance to our age. From each of the four Gospel accounts, we learn something new about the character and intentions of Joseph. Let's examine each portrait separately.

Matthew's account is succinct and concise in that he paints everything we need to know about Joseph in four short brushstrokes—four verses that create a compelling picture. We learn that Joseph was a rich man, an honorable man, and therefore an unlikely disciple. Yet he uses his wealth not as a wall to insulate himself from the need, but rather as an opportunity to partner with others to live sacrificially. As we study Matthew's portrait, we see that he's painted Joseph as a man of risk. We see him approaching Pilate and asking for Jesus' body. He is the only disciple left in proximity to Jesus as the others stand at a distance. While we observe the painting, we can't help but think, "Where were Jesus' disciples?" His body was abandoned. However, a new figure, Joseph of Arimathea, emerges from the shadows and embraces the task ahead.

As we move slowly along the gallery, we come across another portrait, painted by Luke. Luke's picture identifies Joseph as a member of the Jewish ruling council, the Sanhedrin. It was this council that not only condemned Jesus throughout his earthly ministry, but sent him to Pilate for a trial and subsequent execution. But, crucially, Luke points out that Joseph was not part of the majority vote which condemned Jesus. This is the passage that highlights for me the central character of Joseph. Luke says he was a "good and righteous man" (Luke 23:50). A devout Jew waiting for the Kingdom of God to be established. A man of conscience as well as strength and action when an injustice is being perpetrated. I see him standing up for the minority and for justice.

While the Pharisees and Sadducees conformed to the opinions of the majority, Joseph was longing for the Messiah to come and restore his relationship with Israel. He was anticipating the Messiah transforming the earthly fortunes of God's chosen people, which is why Joseph had the courage to go to Pilate to ask for Jesus' body. Moreover, Joseph owned the tomb that he lends Jesus, and he is prepared to make himself unclean by touching a dead body. At great risk to his own life, Joseph gives the body the burial it deserves; it is the upright thing to do.

We then move on to the next portrait. It's much smaller than the others, and it's by a man named Mark (Mark 15:42-47). Although the picture is smaller, it is full of detail and with more precise brush strokes than the other paintings. Mark paints his portrait emphasizing that Joseph was a prominent member of the Sanhedrin council who remained a quiet admirer of Jesus during Jesus' earthly life; yet after Jesus' death, he boldly associated with Jesus. The man who claimed and buried the dead body of Jesus was scared to associate with him during his life. Mark's portrait highlights Joseph's humanity by displaying his fear of others' opinions and judgments. Through Mark's portrait, we can see the great risk that Joseph took in stepping forward.

At the end of the gallery, we come across one more painting by a man named John. John's portrait contains details that the other pictures don't have—two extra brush strokes, particularly in regard to the burial of Jesus' body (John 19:38-42). First, John describes how Jesus was buried with spices: a total of seventy-five pounds of myrrh and aloes. These were spices of such value that even the most prominent and wealthy would consider them extravagant. Additionally, there is another figure painted in this picture. His name is Nicodemus, and he was also a secret disciple. We have seen him before. In a darker picture, perhaps at night (John 3:1-10)?

If we step back and look at the full canvas of John's Gospel, we would see an encounter between Nicodemus and Jesus.

Nicodemus came to Jesus at night and had a conversation with the Galilean rabbi that changed his life forever (John 3:1-10). Though Nicodemus desperately wanted to know Jesus and to understand His message, he knew that publicly associating with Jesus would destroy his reputation. So, Jesus met him where he was at, not judging him for his secrecy; rather, Jesus patiently answered his questions and shared truth with him. The impact Jesus had on Nicodemus during that encounter was enough for him to believe in and follow Christ, even as the majority was yelling to crucify him. Despite the angry populists yelling and crowding around him, Nicodemus would remain resolute in the light because of an encounter that he had with Jesus in the dark.

We read elsewhere in John that, although some wanted Jesus arrested, others were inspired by his messages, claiming that "No one ever spoke like this man!" (John 7:46). The chief priests and Pharisees, however, wanted Jesus arrested due to heresy. But Nicodemus, knowing Jesus' innocence said, "Does our law judge a man without first giving him a hearing and learning what he does?" (John 7:51). We see here that Nicodemus believed in due process, and we also see that Nicodemus stood up for truth even when it was difficult and no one was standing with him. Jesus was not arrested at this time, and I believe that Nicodemus speaking up fulfilled a divine purpose in Jesus' continued earthly ministry.

In John's Gospel, we see portraits of two secret disciples using their privilege and position to fight for justice. We see two influential, respected men standing against the mob on behalf of a man who changed their lives with his love, hope, and truth. We see men who went against the majority, prepared to deal with the backlash because they'd had an encounter with Jesus.

* * *

From the portraits that I have described on the easels of all four Gospel writers, I see Joseph of Arimathea as a good and upright man who was not a part of the majority who condemned Jesus. His picture shows a standout member of the Sanhedrin willing to risk it all, to be ridiculed and rejected for what he believes. As I've studied and pondered the Gospel accounts of Joseph for many months, I'm intrigued that Joseph took responsibility for someone that was not himself. He took responsibility for the other, setting aside his interests and possessions.

What strikes me most as we survey the portraiture of Joseph is this heart that he clearly had for other people. This is the defining feature of Joseph of Arimathea; it is as if he is embodying the philosophy of the French philosopher Emmanuel Levinas who said that he sees in another person's face a reflection of himself. He sees the individual's brokenness, pain, and longings—the uncertainties and anxiety in their faces—reflecting his own fears and pain. Like Levinas, Joseph sees the humanity and the glory of people even when the majority seeks to villainize and dehumanize them.[2] He would not be part of our contemporary paradigm whereby the elderly or other social groups are "othered," treated as intrinsically different from and foreign to oneself.

Joseph associated himself with a dead man, an insurrectionist in the eyes of Rome. He did not "other" Him. He walked away from his prestigious lifestyle and moved towards a man who was no longer the hoped-for Messiah, but rather just another fallen wonder-worker. Yet Joseph stood up for this man when it counted,

> WE ARE LOOKING NOT AT A SPIRITUAL GIANT OR A HERO OF THE FAITH AS MENTIONED IN THE HEBREWS HALL OF FAME, BUT AT A SIMPLE BUSINESSPERSON WHO HAD ENCOUNTERED THE GOD WHO SPOKE FOR THE MOST ORDINARY OF PEOPLE.

giving his all to serve the One who came to serve us all and give His life as a ransom for many (Matthew 20:28).

The portraits of Joseph's life speak to us all, with easel after easel demonstrating something of relevance to our everyday context and lives. We are looking not at a spiritual giant or a hero of the faith as mentioned in the Hebrews hall of fame, but at a simple businessperson who had encountered the God who spoke for the most ordinary of people.

It might not be on a canvas with paint. It might be in the classroom, in the boardroom, or at home with your children, but I urge and invite you to walk through the gallery with me. To look at the exhibition of Joseph's life with fresh eyes and to lean into the story of a person of the small print who has captivated me and, I pray, will captivate you. I believe that amidst this gallery of portraits, you will find your own story.

02

A GREAT RESPONSIBILITY

Joseph of Arimathea, a prominent member of the
Council . . .
- Mark 15:43, NIV

In my time as a special adviser to the Prime Minister of the UK, I had the privilege of working with some of the most senior civil servants responsible for executing government policy. During a recent visit by John Maxwell, a commanding voice when it comes to developing leaders and teaching leadership, I introduced him to some of these senior civil servants. When working with leaders, I always like to take the opportunity to enable and encourage them to exercise distinctive Christian leadership in the workplace. Which is why we gathered together, in the prominent building of Her Majesty's Treasury. It was a great opportunity to introduce

John and his insights to a very influential group of people. I distinctly remember John explaining to them that the higher up you went within an organization, the more important it was to understand the pressures of prominence and the expectations imposed on you by others. When you are a person of prominence, your voice carries extra weight, and your opinions are listened to with greater focus. John described this process in terms of a triangle, broad at the bottom but narrowing as it reaches closer the top. As individuals became more prominent, others, in greater number, became more dependent on their judgments. The more you rise, the more influence you have.

I imagine that Joseph of Arimathea, by virtue of his prominence, would have had many people depending on him and looking up to him. Perhaps, as often happens with all leaders, they would have looked with an eye of jealousy, but also with admiration. Every decision and every move was scrutinized and judged due to his powerful position. Of the little we know of Joseph, we do know he was a prominent member of the Sanhedrin Council. Joseph would have been educated in the Hebrew scriptures and would have undertaken years of rigorous study, sitting under a prominent rabbi. It is said that you become like those you spend time with. For Joseph, this meant he would have spent the majority of his time with a group who was highly concerned about maintaining order so as not to lose the power and autonomy they possessed. The council was an assembly of seventy-one rabbis appointed to sit as a tribunal in every city in the

THE MORE YOU RISE, THE MORE INFLUENCE YOU HAVE.

land of Israel. To be on the Sanhedrin council meant that you were in a position of prominence. Many scholars and historians described the Sanhedrin as the great law court of rulers, elders, and scribes. In other words, it was the supreme theocratic court of the Jews. The council met daily, governing a variety of issues as it pertained to law and order. But perhaps one of the biggest responsibilities of the Sanhedrin was the identification and confirmation of the Messiah.

The Gospel writers identify a delegation from the council going out to question John the Baptist as to whether he was the coming and much expected Messiah (Matthew 3:1-17). There were many false Messiahs roaming around during the first part of the century deceiving the people and making claims for their own divinity. It was the responsibility of the council to identify and denounce them. And they took their jobs seriously.

The members of the Sanhedrin council largely believed that Jesus' claims to be the Messiah were false. They were concerned about the havoc that followed in the wake of anywhere Jesus went. People flocked to him and hung on his every word. He was a radical, and his teachings threatened the order that the Sanhedrin sought to maintain. But, as the Gospel writers tell us, Joseph did not agree with the rest of the council about the person of Jesus: the council said Jesus' words were blasphemous, but Joseph thought otherwise. He silently followed Jesus, not wanting to lose his position, reputation, and prominence. He feared what would happen if he publicly proclaimed his devotion; he was cautious, not wanting to lose his influence.

When I look at Joseph, I see someone who is a steward of

his influence. To be a steward of influence requires humility to temper prominence.

I recall a conversation with Rick Warren, who I first met during the Global World Economic Forum in Switzerland twenty years ago. This was before he released *Purpose Driven Life*, a book which has influenced millions of people. Rick and I were sitting in a coffee shop, thinking about the Christian contribution to the debates taking place at the forum regarding the future of politics and economics. I was very struck by his concern for ensuring that people had values which would underwrite their lives and give them purpose. Amongst a gathering of such high-powered people, we were discussing the importance of stewarding the gifts God had given us and the people around us, particularly stressing the different ways in which influence and affluence have the ability to change people's attitudes and values. Affluence can be easily stewarded with generosity in giving or tithing. It is influence that is more difficult to steward.

The importance of stewarding our influence is explained in the most famous sermon ever preached, the Sermon on the Mount (Matthew 5:13-16). Jesus said to his listeners: "You are the salt of the earth." We, as followers of Jesus, are called to be enhancers and preservers. This stewarding needs to take place within the context of very real humility. Remember Jesus' comments when he called his disciples

AFFLUENCE CAN BE EASILY STEWARDED WITH GENEROSITY IN GIVING OR TITHING. IT IS INFLUENCE THAT IS MORE DIFFICULT TO STEWARD.

together and said, "You know that the rulers of the Gentiles lord it over them, and their great ones exercise authority over them" (Matthew 20:25). But, looking at the disciples, he tells them not to

> WE LEARN FROM JOSEPH THAT WE NEED TO ACCEPT OUR OWN PROMINENCE THAT IS FOUND IN THE EVERYDAY.

be like that. Joseph was God-fearing and, I'll assume, he would have recognized his prominence as a gift from God. His humility marked him out from the rest of the crowd.

We learn from Joseph that we need to accept our own prominence that is found in the everyday. Maybe it's the mother who plans the children's extracurricular activities, the president of a university society, or the father who organizes sports on a Saturday morning. The hidden figures who are rarely found on a stage, but are working hard behind the scenes, are the lifeblood for those in the spotlight. It could be having a voice in an influential think tank where your opinions and ideas might be used, but no one will see you to give you the credit. People with extraordinary gifts and talents, used in a way that's not visible in public, but invaluable when used in private. People of the small print.

Like Joseph, it is probable that in certain circles you are in the spotlight, and in others you play a more behind-the-scenes role. Whether your prominence and leadership are more behind the scenes or in the spotlight, the fact remains that you have people relying on you and, similarly to Joseph, you have a decision to make regarding whether you will humbly use your prominence for good or let pride consume you. While in positions of prominence, it is easy to become consumed by moving up, holding more power, and having greater influence. Whether your sphere of influence is big or small, it is important to retain humility in positions of leadership.

We must also recognize that God has called certain people to a prominence in leadership and they stand out as a result. With any kind of spotlight, the pressures become insurmountable. We are harsh on our politicians, our church leaders, and our business leaders. Their prominence is usually explained away by their desire for power, financial reward, or influence, which seems to legitimize any attack upon them. *The higher you climb the harder you will fall* is a truism strongly (and unfortunately) held for our generation. I would urge caution. We are always leading and following simultaneously. To be a good leader, be a good follower first. Joseph was a leader in the Sanhedrin court, but he was still under the authority of the law, and under Roman occupation, the *pax romana* was the ultimate authority over the people. So, when we look at someone more prominent than ourselves, let's try to ensure that our first reaction is to bless, to understand, and to sympathize with compassion.

TO BE A GOOD LEADER, BE A GOOD FOLLOWER FIRST.

God never gives a leader an easy task. When in the Bible did God give someone an easy job? Free from criticism and opposition? It is never easy to move people or a vision forward. People who are prominent are under immense amounts of pressure. They possess strengths which are vulnerable to temptation, especially if the leader becomes stressed. Leaders and people in positions of prominence need our prayers now more than ever. We must ask God to protect and safeguard the blind spots and weaknesses that even the best leaders carry. This is why Paul urged Timothy to pray for leaders: "First of all, then, I urge that supplications, prayers, intercessions, and thanksgivings be made for all people, for kings and all who are in high positions, that we may lead a peaceful and quiet life, godly and dignified in every way. This is good, and it is pleasing in the sight of God our Savior" (1 Timothy 2:1-3).

PRIDE, LIKE INFLUENCE, CAN SPREAD LIKE WILDFIRE.

We are often tempted to look for ways to fast track us to greater influence and impact. Perhaps a center-fold spread on our accomplishments or a broadcasting network to focus on our accolades. A choir of affirmation that cheers from a distance, without knowing the character of the person to whom they sing. A spike in followers on social media. Such attention whispers and taunts. Pride, like influence, can spread like wildfire. Jesus warns us about such dangers. He calls pride a trap and He urges us to consider how we deal with it, as well as how to conduct ourselves when we are in the midst of such prominence.

After the people saw the many miracles that Jesus performed throughout His life, they began to say, "This is indeed the Prophet who is to come into the world!" (John 6:14). Five thousand men plus women and children proclaimed wonder and awe at Jesus the prophet. Thousands of voices swelling into a roar of ovation and adulation for all his deeds. I can't imagine for a minute Jesus didn't hear their cries and become tempted by power and pride. A chorus promising power and prominence can intoxicate. No cross needed. No sacrifice required. An army of disciples and followers waiting in anticipation for His next instruction.

Jesus heard the voices. He heard the cries. But He also heard someone else—the voice of His Father. And when He heard Him, Jesus retreated and sought his face. Jesus withdrew to be by Himself. He preferred to be alone with the true God who could direct Him rather than sit with a crowd who would promote Him. Jesus knew prominence was a means to carry forth His Father's mission. But He understood that it wasn't the end goal. Logic didn't tell Him to dismiss the crowds. Nor was it conventional wisdom that told Him to turn his back on a willing audience. It wasn't an audible opinion or expectation from an external source. It was a voice from within.

So we must ask ourselves the question: if we are in a position of prominence, do we set aside time to listen to the voice of God? Do we wait on Him to show us how to use our position and power for his Kingdom? Do we concern ourselves with the needs of the lost, the last, and the least? If we pigeonhole individuals who are not as prominent or established as we are, then we permit ourselves to treat them however we see fit in our own eyes and not as God sees them. Humanity is prone to different types of pecking orders, to hierarchy, and to positions of influence. Whether it's by prioritizing the privileged over the destitute or giving opportunities to the affluent over the poor, if we are not careful, an impassable gulf can be created that can be almost impossible to bridge.

Jesus' approach to prominence is a model to us: He was humble and used His influence to serve others. He was inclusive in His interaction with individuals; He didn't exclude or isolate people. He socialized with the wealthy. Jesus laid hands on the blind and declared healing over the lame. He interacted with the social outcasts and spent time with notable sinners. Skin disease couldn't keep Him from the lepers, and racial divides couldn't stop Him from speaking to a Samaritan woman. Jesus instructs us to look upon people with the same eyes that we look through at ourselves. He asks us to listen to the still, small voice of the Holy Spirit who speaks life, value, and worth to every individual that we encounter.

Jesus' life and ministry sent a clear, unmistakable message to people of prominence and people of influence: your position does not mean you can stand in a state of superiority over others. On the contrary, it calls you to serve them. If you are in a position of leadership, management, or influence, you are instructed to change the way that you look at people. Not to see them as insider or outsider, but to see everyone as human. There's equal standing at the foot of the cross.

The same voice that prompted Joseph of Arimathea not to be part of the prevailing worldview is a voice that is also available to us. It's available for us to take heed and respond to. When you are prominent, pride becomes a temptation which relentlessly knocks upon your door. Yet, from my experience in my Christian walk, Jesus rarely thuds down the

> **IF YOU ARE IN A POSITION OF LEADERSHIP, MANAGEMENT, OR INFLUENCE, YOU ARE INSTRUCTED TO CHANGE THE WAY THAT YOU LOOK AT PEOPLE.**

door. Instead, He gently knocks and waits: "Behold, I stand at the door and knock. If anyone hears my voice and opens the door, I will come in to him and eat with him, and he with me" (Revelation 3:20).

In a world that's getting busier and more complicated by the day, which voice do you choose to hear? Few people and even fewer *prominent* people allow themselves the space or the time to sit in the silence and hear His voice. Even fewer tend to open the door. Amidst the competing demands and fleeting pleasures which prominence can bring, the timeless promise of His presence is calling and inviting us in. There is no prominent position or seat of prestige and importance where the voice of Jesus cannot be heard if we humbly listen.

That was true for Joseph of Arimathea. Whether it was the intense debates in the Sanhedrin court, the insensitive interruptions which he must have faced, or the incredible demands on his time, Joseph heard the still, small voice urging him to pursue a relationship with Jesus Christ. He obeyed the voice that convicted him that Jesus was the long-awaited Messiah.

We don't know when, but at some point, in the midst of his prominence, Joseph was convinced that a day was soon to come when every other voice would be silenced. A day when Jesus' voice and His voice only would be heard. A voice that held more weight than the opinions of others, and a voice that would echo throughout eternity.

03

THE RICH MAN

*When it was evening, there came a rich man from
Arimathea, named Joseph . . .*
- Matthew 27:57

I remember being asked by a thoughtful non-believer at university in South Africa whether, in the teaching of Jesus, it was the poor who would have a monopoly of heaven. And I still contemplate that question today.

Having spent over forty years in the center of finance in London, I've had to deal with money every day of my life. I know few things as clearly as I know the captivating power that money has.

Not only the power it has over the rich, but also over people across the board. I have met billionaires with huge possessions who are faithful stewards of their wealth. I have met impoverished young people whose few possessions had an extraordinary grip on their lives—so much so as to deflect them from a true relationship with Jesus.

Whenever I've been asked the question over the last forty years, about whether it's possible to be wealthy (or more precisely a banker) and be a Christian, the answer I give is the same as given by Jesus: "it is easier for a camel to go through the eye of a needle than for a rich person to enter the kingdom of God" (Matthew 19:24). There is a real

IF YOU ARE GRIPPED BY POSSESSIONS, YOU WILL GROPE PURPOSELESSLY FOR MEANING.

responsibility on those who do have possessions to know *who* possesses whom: do your possessions, your prestige, your finances, your prominence guide you, or do you guide them? If you are gripped by possessions, you will grope purposelessly for meaning. Possessions are subordinate to the great relationships that Jesus calls us to—the relationship with Him, His Father, the Spirit, and the people around us. In relationship with Jesus, we recover a power that is latent and strong—a power that can drive riches into the proper subordinate position in our lives.

I often think of the rich young ruler in Matthew's Gospel. I've heard many sermons preached on his encounter with Jesus over the years. The young ruler was rich and prestigious—and he knew it. "Teacher," he asked, "what good deed must I do to have eternal life?" (Matthew 19:16). In other words, thinking like a business person: how much do I need to invest to be certain of my return? Jesus' answer was intended to make the young man recoil: "If you would be perfect, go, sell what you possess and give to the poor, and you will have treasure in heaven; and come, follow me" (Matthew 19:21).

The statement left the young man distraught. It wasn't the money that hindered the rich man but the self-sufficiency and lack of dependence on Christ. The young man thought that his salvation was just a check away. He thought it was a transactional. He worked hard, he paid his dues, he earned his money, and with his good deeds, his account could be credited as paid in full. Jesus essentially said: "Not a chance. Before you come follow me, you must give up what you treasure most. What you ask for costs more than you own, and more than you can afford to pay." You can't use a financial system to pay for the debt you owe. You need a savior to pay it for you.

The rich man's priorities were revealed through his response: he walked away dejected. Hosea 13:6 describes this tragic gulf between the man's intentions and what he claims to want: "Being satisfied, their heart became proud; therefore, they forgot me" (NASB). If we aren't guarded when we become prosperous, we become proud—and then we often forget God.

How hard is it to enter the Kingdom of God when you are rich? It is very difficult for the person who is prosperous to learn that they cannot pay for something priceless. And we need to be clear that being prosperous is relative. It does not only refer to the über-rich, but all of us who have possessions which are far greater than the majority of people living in our world today. In the Sermon on the Mount, Jesus' opening beatitude addressed his listeners, saying, "Blessed are the poor in Spirit" (Matthew 5:3). The true pearl of great price is given not to those who are self-sufficient but to the spiritually bankrupt, the ones who understand their need for a savior. God's reward is given to those who truly surrender, rich or poor. The people who don't brag about what they can bring to the table, but those who beg for mercy and pardon. It's a strange kingdom when salvation is born in the dirty soil of destitution and dependency rather than the fertile ground of riches and success.

Joseph understood his need for a savior well. The great strength of Joseph of Arimathea was not purely what wealth he had, but what he was prepared to do with that wealth—and not just functionally but relationally. Joseph of Arimathea was a man with money, but he was not a lover of money. "For the love of money is a root of all kinds of evils. It is through this craving that some have wandered away from the faith and pierced themselves with many pangs" (1 Timothy 6:10). The lesson we learn from Joseph is that, though he was rich, he was not stumbling in his wealth, but rather, he was stewarding his affluence. Through his wealth, he was able to afford the very tomb in which Jesus was buried. He used his wealth to build up and honor others, rather than selfishly using it on his own interests. Although he may have been a secret

> IT'S A STRANGE KINGDOM WHEN SALVATION IS BORN IN THE DIRTY SOIL OF DESTITUTION AND DEPENDENCY RATHER THAN THE FERTILE GROUND OF RICHES AND SUCCESS.

disciple, when the time came, he laid everything down in order to follow Jesus. Through this we see that Joseph of Arimathea was a great steward of his affluence.

This is very important for every disciple who is in the blessed position of having possessions greater than those that are needed for ordinary life—and most likely, that would include every reader of this book. The stewarding of affluence and the careful use of finance is a major issue for every Christian. Generosity is the hallmark of our faith, and it is a hallmark of our time. Whether it's the amount of time and energy that we spend with others who need our help or the use of finances as part of our discipleship, we should be known for our generosity.

Paul told Timothy, "Command those who are rich in this present world not to be arrogant nor to put their hope in wealth, which is so uncertain, but to put their hope in God, who richly provides us with everything for our enjoyment" (1 Timothy 6:17, NIV). Prosperity is a common consequence of our stewardship over what we have and our everyday faithfulness. Paul didn't tell the rich to feel guilty about being rich; he warned them of its dangers. We would do well to remember not to get tangled up in

> WE CAN OFTEN FORGET HOW GENEROUS GOD WAS AND CONTINUES TO BE TO US.

it. If you and I stockpile earthly treasures and not eternal, heavenly ones, what does that say about where we put our trust and where we focus our attention?

We can often forget how generous God was and continues to be to us. God made the first move of generosity by sending his son

Jesus to die on a cross. God the Father went above and beyond anything we could deserve or imagine, generously forgiving us. Generously accepting us. Generously loving us. Every breath that we take is a gift from a generous Father to His children.

If we forget that everything from God is a gift, our possessions and wealth can easily become idols to us. We live with open hands, trusting that God will provide for us. If we hold on too tightly to our wealth we become slaves to it. But when we are generous, we become more fulfilled, free, and satisfied. God knows the good that can come from stewarding our wealth well and living a radical life of generosity with the prosperity we have. Although it's contrary to our nature, the source of generosity urges us to give, because every time we make an investment, that investment is being registered in our eternal home.

> IF WE FORGET THAT EVERYTHING FROM GOD IS A GIFT, OUR POSSESSIONS AND WEALTH CAN EASILY BECOME IDOLS TO US.

There are many ways that we can invest in eternity on this side of heaven. One of the ways that we can guard our hearts against pride and love of money is to live by this biblical principle of generosity: Love first, receive second. This leads to contagious generosity. God loved us so much that He gave us His best. Loving first, receiving love in return from us second. This generosity can be found throughout the scriptures. When the love of God through Jesus appeared, He saved us. Not because of anything we had done, but because of His grace and mercy, through the washing of rebirth and renewal by the Holy Spirit whom He generously poured out upon us through Jesus (Titus 3:4-6).

It's apparent that generosity is an irresistible and irreplaceable quality of spirituality. Inside every person is a deep-seated, God-given desire to live out a generous life. Generosity is essential to walking with Jesus. What Jesus expects us to do in life cannot be done without a generous attitude. We can give without loving, but we cannot love without giving. We are most like Jesus when we are generous, investing in eternity.

Of course, I do not want to oversimplify the terribly difficult and complicated issues of capitalism and the systems that distribute wealth. I understand that we cannot just clap our hands or snap our fingers and assume the money will flow easily. We live within structures and systems, policies and programs. However, the Bible is clear that God's storehouse is fully stocked. The problem is not in the supply but rather it is in the distribution of that supply. He invites us to live out our lives by investing in the next generation.

WE ARE MOST LIKE JESUS WHEN WE ARE GENEROUS, INVESTING IN ETERNITY.

Many American families who lived in the South during the Civil War had accumulated large amounts of Confederate currency. Thanks to a variety of variables, families became convinced that the South was going to lose and their money would soon be worth nothing. As a result, many families decided to put all their money into the currency that was to come and prepare themselves for a future at the end of the war. Despite the hardships of war, families had to constantly believe that the investments they were making into the coming currency would be worth the present sacrifice.[3]

In the same way, we are encouraged to invest in a currency which is to come: the currency of heaven. Are you investing in this currency? Do you believe the exchange rate is better than anything this world has to offer?

We are often tempted to succumb to the idol of more, and to trust *more* over God. Yet more can be a cruel master in that it causes us to drink from broken cisterns which never fully satisfy (Jeremiah 2:13). Everything we acquire on earth—if it's not invested in the Kingdom—will eventually lose its value. The currency of heaven is the deposit that Jesus has made in each and every believer. It's up to us what we choose to do with that deposit. Will we be like Joseph and build the Kingdom, or will we betray the Kingdom, like Judas did, for thirty pieces of silver?

God asks us to be faithful with what we have and trust Him with what He provides, rather than being greedy or stingy. If you and I hoard earthly treasure and not heavenly ones, what does that say about where we put our trust? Money is a rotten ruler. It rusts and it rots. It loses its value and joy. It never satisfies. Selfishness and greed can have a growling, insatiable stomach, hungering for more and more. But feed it, and we risk more than losing what we have. We risk losing purpose.

> **EVERYTHING WE ACQUIRE ON EARTH—IF IT'S NOT INVESTED IN THE KINGDOM—WILL EVENTUALLY LOSE ITS VALUE.**

* * *

I have often been captured by the image of the early church in Acts 2:46: "And day by day, attending the temple together and breaking bread in their homes, they received their food with glad and generous hearts." Generosity through financial investment is not the only way that we invest in eternity. We can invest in the Kingdom of Heaven through our hospitality. We need to reawaken this verse in the hearts of our society now more than ever. We are a fast and furious society. Though we have become more efficient in practice, we have lost the personal connection. Our culture is set up for isolation. We wear headphones when we commute. We communicate via text messages. We no longer have to actively exert energy to engage in a conversation. We can fill up our gas tank with a card from the pump. We can make bank deposits online. We can buy a gift on Amazon without having to speak to a customer service representative. You can get to the end of your day without speaking to anybody. Yet, by the power of the Holy Spirit, Jesus wants us to be the exception. To actively engage in hospitality and concern for others.

The first Christians met together daily in the temple and in one another's homes. The house, the place of belonging, was the primary means and method of the church. This was a brilliant strategy of God. The first generation was a melting pot of different cultures and backgrounds. Historians tell us at least eighteen different nationalities heard Peter's inaugural sermon on the Day of Pentecost. Jews stood next to Gentiles. The rich next to the poor. Men next to the women.

Can the same diversity be said about us today? All of us can be hospitable. We can all sit around a table. Hospitality opens the door to uncommon communion with others. You can issue a genuine invitation. To the co-worker who eats at the staff lunchroom alone. To the new worker who has just moved into the city from another country. We are investing in a different kind of community when we invest in hospitality to others. Generosity and heavenly currency extends beyond what we do with our money while on earth; we must be generous with our time, with our love, and with our empathy. For all the promises we think wealth and individualism make, they cannot keep a single one for eternity. Relationships, sharing truth with people, living for Jesus on the earth—these are things that have an eternal legacy, an everlasting impact.

> **HOSPITALITY OPENS THE DOOR TO UNCOMMON COMMUNION WITH OTHERS.**

Joseph understood this. He gave his time and efforts to make sure Jesus received an honorable burial. He used his wealth to pay for the borrowed tomb of Jesus. He gave what he had for a greater cause that was other than his own. And he got to participate in an eternal project that was worth more than anything he had in his pocket.

We are invited to do the same with what we have and with the time we have. As you and I are obedient and faithful to invest our talents, then God will give the increase (1 Corinthians 3:7). You have more on deposit than you know. You are more prosperous than you realize. Let's emulate Joseph. He didn't let the itch for acquiring more things or more wealth derail him from using what he had for eternal Kingdom purposes. The investment from Jesus has been made. The currency has been deposited. It is up to us to use it and invest it wisely.

The character, heart, and generosity of Joseph laid the foundation for his actions leading up to and following Jesus' death. Unassuming and faithful, Joseph begins fulfilling his purpose as a disciple of the Messiah. A Messiah for whom he has patiently waited.

04

THE WAITING ROOM

He himself was waiting for the kingdom of God.
- Luke 23:51, NIV

Our society doesn't like to wait. We're busy people. We've got schedules to keep, things to do, and we're always in a hurry. We're the get-up-and-go generation. We weave through the traffic, looking for a faster lane. We frown at the person who takes eleven items into the ten-item express checkout. We tap our toe while we wait to receive our pre-ordered Starbucks seconds after entering the shop. We want minute rice in thirty seconds. We want six-pack abs in six minutes. Delay has become a dirty word. We don't like to wait. Not for the doctor or for a delivery, for traffic, or for God. Unforeseen circumstances beyond our control can throw us off course and subject us to a time of waiting, to a time when our plans are overruled.

When things don't go according to our wishes or people don't fit our expectations, we tend to lose patience and become overwhelmed.

We all go through seasons in God's waiting room. The young couple seated in the corner? They are waiting to get pregnant. That gentleman with the briefcase who has sent out hundreds of résumés? He's waiting on a job. As the clock ticks, hours become days, days become weeks, weeks become months, months become years. Waiting on God to intervene, waiting on God to interrupt, waiting on God with hope. We are caught in this tension, and we find ourselves stuck in God's waiting room.

Joseph of Arimathea was familiar with God's waiting room. He was expectantly waiting, like so many Orthodox Jews, for the promised Messiah. Though there was no single understanding of what the Messiah would be like, there were common elements of His coming which every Jew would have assumed within their messianic expectations. He was to institute a renewal of the Temple in Jerusalem. It was also commonly understood that the Messiah would be a royal military leader who would overthrow Israel's enemies and prove His Lordship through conquest. The long-awaited Messiah was not expected to promote peace and to die at the hands of the Roman authorities. As British scholar N.T. Wright suggests, "A Messiah who died at the hands of the pagans, instead of winning God's battle against

> WAITING ON GOD TO INTERVENE, WAITING ON GOD TO INTERRUPT, WAITING ON GOD WITH HOPE. WE ARE CAUGHT IN THIS TENSION, AND WE FIND OURSELVES STUCK IN GOD'S WAITING ROOM.

them, was a deceiver."[4]

Joseph's expectations of God and the coming Messiah originated from the cultural framework in which he participated. It's vital to remember that the Kingdom of God for which he was waiting was not some rabbinic invention or a resolution of the council of the elders conceived in that time. It was the long, explicit, scriptural expression of a redeeming salvific activity of a person who would be Yeshua, who would be Messiah.

In light of this worldview and embedded within its tradition, Joseph had a settled and fixed expectation and hope that this Kingdom could come at any moment. However, what Joseph could not have imagined was the way in which this Kingdom would be inaugurated in and through the life of Jesus. I can imagine him grappling with a developing reality of Jesus' authority and influence and the growth in his own personal trust in Jesus Christ against the context of this waiting. Jesus didn't quite line up with his expectations. Nonetheless, Joseph was captivated by Jesus' claims to this expectant but undefined Kingdom. His expectations and ideas were being challenged as he became engrossed by the person of Jesus. Joseph waited upon God and because of that, he discovered the Messiah who he had been waiting for his whole life. Joseph's views did not align with other prominent Jews—his co-workers and colleagues—which is why he was a secret disciple during Jesus' life. He was processing the fact that he had to leave behind his expectations of the coming Messiah in order to recognize Jesus as the expectant liberator.

Like Joseph, our own expectations often collide with reality precisely because of our selective reading of the situations we are in. How often have we had to correct our own images of Jesus, expecting Him to dance to our tunes, only to realize, when He doesn't anoint our desires for self-satisfaction or fulfillment, we have defined Him in our own image? Our view of God often limits our understanding of the fullness of His character.

Unlike Joseph, we know the full expression of what the messianic promises were. We have seen in Jesus the fulfillment of all that expectation. Now we can act and wait for the final revelation. During this waiting for the second coming of Christ, we can sometimes grow impatient and frustrated as we try to fulfill our divine purpose on earth.

There was a season in which I saw several of my financier friends becoming full-time Christian ministers. So, I too began a period of pursuing discernment, trying to assess whether I was similarly called. In many ways, I longed for that to happen. I went to visit the Archbishop of Cape Town in South Africa (where I was born). He was a remarkable man of God who initiated a new outpouring of the Spirit of God in the church in South Africa. I still have his letter in which he offered to ordain me as a priest in his diocese. It was a confusing time; I didn't know whether to accept his offer for ordination or continue my career as a banker.

A year passed as I was praying to discern God's will, and I was waiting for the Spirit of God to clarify my next steps and the main directional thrust of my life. I decided to set aside a day to pray, fast, and to walk along the River Thames outside London. As I did so, I had the closest assurance I have ever had that my calling was to remain in finance. The call to priesthood was attractive, and it felt like a huge sacrifice giving it up. As I walked along the path of the river, I realized that obedience

WAITING IS NOT WASTING.

is better than sacrifice, and as harsh as the financial environment is, His grace would be sufficient to equip me. And then, an extraordinary verse from Luke 24 leapt out at me. Taken completely out of its context, it had a riveting meaning and was one of the very few occasions that I can absolutely say that I know for a fact that God spoke to me in a decisive way through the Scriptures. It said, "Stay in the city until you are clothed with power from on high" (Luke 24:49). I remained in the city of London and in the financial district specifically—itself called the City—and in retrospect it was in the long waiting that God recalibrated my aspirations, reset my expectations, and reignited my purpose.

Waiting is not wasting. There are times in all our lives when it is not immediately obvious how God intends to move in our lives. Joseph of Arimathea did not waste his time in waiting for the

LEARNING PATIENCE AND WAITING FOR GOD TO REVEAL HIMSELF IN OUR LIVES IS THE DAILY EXPECTATION OF EVERY CHRISTIAN.

Kingdom. He saw the glimpse of it in Jesus, even if he did not fully understand what it was all about. He didn't waste his time, and while he was waiting, he did not waver in his search for the truth. He waited for the Lord to make Himself known to him.

Learning patience and waiting for God to reveal Himself in our lives is the daily expectation of every Christian. We wait for the Kingdom to be fully revealed to us, but we know that the Spirit of God has come. As Luke records Jesus saying in Luke 11:20: "But if it is by the finger of God that I cast out demons, then the kingdom of God has come upon you." In this decisive verse, Jesus gives us the Kingdom. In one sense, the waiting experienced by Joseph is over. In another, the fulfillment is yet to come. The Messiah came and died for us and gave us the Holy Spirit as a deposit for what is to come (2 Corinthians 1:22). But we still experience pain, suffering, sin, and separation from God while on the earth; we wait for Jesus to come back so that we can be united with God. We live in this in-between age of uncertainty, of doubt, of misunderstanding, of disappointment. But that does not weigh us down as we wait for the full expression of the Kingdom of God, when sorrow, weeping, and mourning will cease.

In one of the most dramatic examples of waiting in the Bible, Daniel prays for people who had been oppressed for seventy years. He abstained from food and drink for twenty-one days as he labored in prayer, persisted, pleaded, and agonized. No response.

On the twenty-second day, an angel of God appeared. He revealed to Daniel that his prayer had been heard on the first day. From an earthly perspective, nothing was happening for the first twenty-one days. But, from a heavenly perspective, a battle was raging in the spiritual realm. Daniel's waiting was not wasted. God was working!

What if Daniel had given up, lost faith, or walked away from God? He might not have experienced the abundant life that God had for him. He might not have seen God's promises fulfilled in his life. Daniel's patience is an example to us. We must walk out in our purpose, relying on and believing in God's promises.

When we wait, we trust the workings of God. The Hebrew word for wait is *Qavah*, and it has two meanings, both helpful. One is "to bind together." The word picture depicts the image of a person braiding hair or binding the strands of a rope together. But it also means "to look patiently, or to hope, or to expect or to look eagerly."[5] Waiting on God requires confident expectation. We trust someone is binding this thing together, weaving our lives and purpose together. To wait is not to be inactive. To wait is to have a trusting hope that everything will be bound together for a glorious purpose.

The New Testament word for wait is equally helpful: *Prosdechomai*. It is a Greek compound word between *pros*, which means "toward," and *dechomai*, which means "to wait."[6] The grammar is a bit awkward, but the meaning is beautiful. To wait eagerly as if you're on the edge of your seat or standing on your tiptoes. The New Testament uses this word when it talks about a man by the name of Simeon. God told Simeon that he

> TO WAIT IS NOT TO BE INACTIVE. TO WAIT IS TO HAVE A TRUSTING HOPE THAT EVERYTHING WILL BE BOUND TOGETHER FOR A GLORIOUS PURPOSE.

would live long enough to see the birth of the Messiah. Simeon was patient and had faith that God would fulfill what He had promised. When Simeon saw Jesus as a baby, he said, "Sovereign Lord, as you have promised you may now dismiss your servant in peace . . . for my eyes have seen your salvation" (Luke 2:29-30, NIV).

Simeon waited many years for God's promise to be fulfilled in his life, but he continued to have faith in God's promise and rejoiced when it was fulfilled.

To wait is not to be inactive. To wait is not to be passive. It's to wait forwardly. It means living in expectation of God's blessing. To wait is not to worry and panic about what's next. To wait is not to fear nor to make demands. To wait is to live in this faithful, hopeful, and prayerful expectation that God will fulfill His promise.

Think about a farmer. Does he attempt to harvest a crop on the day after planting the seed? No, he plants the seed, and then what does he do? He waits. He may water the field, but he's waiting. Does he run up and down the field saying, "Come on, grow!" No. He has learned to trust the inherent nature of the seed. He has learned that, given time, the seed will shove away the shell and grow. The farmer waits while the seed works. Would you not consider trusting the inherent nature of your Heavenly Father? Would you not consider abandoning the posture of anxiety and choosing instead to live in confident expectation?

The mantra of God's waiting room is this: "Be still and know that I am God" (Psalm 46:10). God told this to Moses and the children of Israel after they had just been released from Egyptian captivity: "And Moses said to the people, 'Fear not, stand firm, and see the salvation of the Lord, which he will work for you today. For the Egyptians whom you see today, you shall never see again'" (Exodus 14:13). The Israelites had the Egyptian army behind them, the Red Sea in front of them. It was death on both sides. It was an impossible situation. But what did God tell them to do?

Stand still. They didn't know God's hand was already beneath the Red Sea, parting the waves. That His breath was already coming from the heavens to separate the water. God was working while they were waiting.

We can be still because God is God. We can be patient because God is active. We can rest because God is busy. We can be glad because God is good, and our good God works. And while we wait, God doesn't just work. He works for us.

In our seasons of waiting, we must also try to remember God's patience with us. How many could say God has been patient with you? When was He patient with you? Was there a season in your life when the only time you mentioned God's name was in vain? Was there a season in your life that the only time you went to church was because someone dragged you there? Was God not patient with you then? Has he not been patient with you even today? If God has been so patient with us, can we not be patient with Him and with His ways? Since God is so patient with us, should we not be patient with others?

> WE CAN STILL BE STILL BECAUSE GOD IS GOD. WE CAN BE PATIENT BECAUSE GOD IS ACTIVE.

Like Joseph, let's be a people who wait upon God with hope and humility. Just as Joseph waited upon God to reveal Himself to Joseph, we must also seek to set aside our expectations of God in order to experience and see Him fully. If you ask, God will grant you the patience, like Joseph of Arimathea, to wait for the Kingdom to come with eyes wide open.

Joseph, expectant of the Kingdom of God to be fulfilled

through the person of Jesus, now has to stand up to the rest of thecouncil and defend this man they seek to destroy.

05

PASSION FOR JUSTICE

He was a good and honorable man . . .
- Luke 23:51

In Luke's account, Joseph of Arimathea refused to go along with the judgment of the ruling council to convict Jesus. The day after Jesus was arrested, "The council of the elders of the people, both the chief priests and the teachers of the law, met together, and Jesus was led before them" (Luke 22:66, NIV). Joseph was there in that council defending Jesus, not denying him. Joseph "had not consented to their decision and action" (Luke 23:51). In this short verse, we see the commitment of Joseph—a commitment to justice, to fairness, and to speaking up even when the crowd was asking for blood. A man standing out against the prevailing consensus. A person of conscience standing alone. Someone who was prepared to put his core values first and not to be drawn along with the irrational intensity of the Sanhedrin and the speeches at their meeting.

Joseph speaks into this partisan invective. The council wanted Jesus crucified, but Joseph knew Jesus was innocent, and he had to stand against this injustice. It was Joseph, a business person and prominent member of the Sanhedrin council, who risked his reputation and position in order to stand up for an innocent man. Though we don't know the grounds of Joseph's argument, he must have argued against the decision to accuse Jesus of blasphemy. In his heart of hearts, hidden disciple or not, Joseph knew that Jesus was innocent, so he spoke against the majority and he defended Jesus. Herein lies a true "good and honorable man," as Luke describes him (Luke 23:50, GNT).

"If you are the messiah," the council said "then tell us" (Luke 22:67, NIV). The Scripture tells us they all asked Jesus, "Are you the Son of God, then?" (Luke 22:70). There was clamor as they shouted their threats; their taunting is hardly that of a dispassionate enquiry. You can feel the snarl in their questions. You can imagine the frowns on their faces, with the contours of their faces becoming more and more exacerbated by this supposed resurrectionist and blasphemer.

Jesus brilliantly answers them: "If I tell you, you would not believe, and if I ask you, you will not answer" (Luke 22:67-68). But then He uses a more indicative tone in verse 69: "From now on, the son of man will be seated at the right hand of the mighty

God" (NIV). Here the hypotheticals stop. He claimed to be the Son of God. He has answered directly. The accusations of Jesus' accusers are verified. "Then they said, 'What further testimony do we need? We have heard it ourselves from his own lips'" (Luke 22:71). Then the council brought Jesus before Pilate, "and they began to accuse him, saying, 'We found this man misleading our nation and forbidding us to give tribute to Caesar, and saying that he himself is Christ, a king.'" (Luke 23:2).

It was now up to the Pilate to decide Jesus' fate. He held the seat of power. He had the choice. He wore the signet ring. Was he going to pardon Jesus or send Him to His death? We can picture Pilate ascending to his seat, looking down on the accused Jesus as He is brought into the room and placed below him. Pilate looks at the lone figure and asks, "Are you the King of the Jews?" (Luke 23:3). Jesus at this point may have lifted His head and looked into the eyes of Pilate. Jesus is calm. Perhaps Pilate studied Jesus' face intently. *Why was there no fight? Why was there no fear? No sense of panic. No desire to plead.*

Jesus knew His hour was upon Him to drink the bitter cup He asked to be taken away from Him in the garden of Gethsemane (Luke 22:42). Jesus replies: "You have said so" (Luke 23:3). No defense. No explanation given. No begging for mercy. No asking for pardon or acquittal. The adroitness of the answer carries salvific weight.

The religious leaders' voices prevailed, and Pilate's pride took precedence. The rhetoric of the council's rationalizations rang louder than perhaps Pilate's conscience. With a compelling argument behind the council, and a silent Messiah standing there, the decision was made. Pilate washed his hands. An innocent man condemned. A Savior rejected. An opportunity ignored. Christ's voice was muted and the voice of the people's representatives, bar one, was heard.

Joseph must have had all of these words ringing in his ears. The scenes just described must have been like a film playing over and over in his mind. Allow yourself to be drawn into this gathering of the most senior religious leaders. Watch them—the council, the chief priests, the teachers of the law—taunting Jesus. Then one man steps forward and has the courage to disagree: he was not part of the majority when the vote came to be taken.

He did that most difficult of things: to speak truth to power. Like Joseph, there will always be a need for someone to speak up for the voiceless. To take the side of the exploited. To try to argue for the rights of those who don't have any. That is why the Bible so frequently talks about the importance of justice: "What does the Lord require of you but to do justice, and to love kindness, and to walk humbly with your God?" (Micah 6:8).

Sometimes it feels like we are the only ones in a sea of people who are standing up for what we believe is right. Being a principled person means having values and convictions and also speaking truth even when no one else around us is. Being principled requires courage and strength even at the risk of losing your

> SOMETIMES IT FEELS LIKE WE ARE THE ONLY ONES IN A SEA OF PEOPLE WHO ARE STANDING UP FOR WHAT WE BELIEVE IS RIGHT.

reputation. Standing up for what is right requires sacrifice, but it ushers in the hope that is everlasting. When we fight for justice, we are living out the truths of the Bible. We are following the example of Joseph who boldly and bravely spoke truth.

* * *

In our daily lives, things like economic inequity, racism, political division, and uncertainty feed our fears. People have discordant opinions about their leaders, about government, and about those in seats of power. Yet, as I study the life of Joseph, it occurs to me that a spirit of uncertainty, division, and fear hung over first-century Palestine also. Israel was ruled by an oppressive regime, typified early on in the Gospels with the account recorded of Herod's massacre of babies. The Roman Empire had a strict stance against people whose faith was exalted above the Roman Emperor. It was an insult to Rome, an indictment upon Nero. There was only one king. There was only one Lord. And His face shone off the silver denarii in an individual's pocket. Against this background, Joseph unknowingly joined the pages of Scripture in his active decision to embrace a costly engagement with God's heart. He decided to battle for justice in the midst of this political, social, and cultural constriction that surrounded him.

This is our challenge as Christians. We do not want to be Christians who sit in an ivory tower of community and theology or live in a vacuum. Edmund Burke once declared, "All that it takes for evil to prosper is for righteous people to do nothing."[7] As followers of Jesus, we have both the privilege and the responsibility to do something when we see injustices. We have the privilege of speaking hope and bringing good news to everyone.

Today, the world lives under a cloud of uncertainty, hopelessness, and division. And yet the gospel continues to transform lives. As Christians, we have the opportunity to leave in our wake the joyful evidence of justice, mercy, freedom, and healing to all people groups that are in need. It is our duty to obey James' command: to be both hearers of the word and doers of the word (James 1:19-26). This is how we display and offer hope to people in a world so desperately in need of hope.

> WE DO NOT WANT TO BE CHRISTIANS WHO SIT IN AN IVORY TOWER OF COMMUNITY AND THEOLOGY OR LIVE IN A VACUUM.

When the theologian Augustine was asked about hope he said, "Hope has two beautiful daughters: anger and courage."[8] Anger at the injustice that is happening all around us and courage to do something, to fight for justice, rather than to ignore it and let it continue to happen.

I am constantly challenged in my walk with Christ, wondering if I am embodying God's heart for the marginalized. Am I allowing the Spirit of God to work and move through me? To care for those in poor situations and hurting places? The homeless and the destitute, the broke and the broken? Am I an effective blend of hope, anger, and courage, so that I can constantly pursue a principled life of justice and mercy? The principles and practices of justice align with the commands and character of Jesus. Yet why don't more Christians stand for justice? Kierkegaard once said, "The difference between an admirer and a follower still remains, no matter where you are. The admirer never makes any true sacrifices. He always plays it safe."[9]

Joseph went from being an admirer to a follower of Jesus. From a shadow disciple to being somebody out in the open. Injustice provoked Joseph to speak up. He knew Jesus was innocent, he believed Jesus was who He said He was, and he spoke up so that an innocent man might not die.

Like a thread woven throughout the fabric of God's heart, all throughout Jesus' ministry, justice was His priority. Justice is mentioned over 400 times in the Bible and is a key concern for God. Justice is part of who He is and what Jesus came to reveal. Justice has always been God's design for His creation. The Holy Spirit alights upon Jesus and anoints Him to bring about the justice of His heavenly Father,

> LIKE A THREAD WOVEN THROUGHOUT THE FABRIC OF GOD'S HEART, ALL THROUGHOUT JESUS' MINISTRY, JUSTICE WAS HIS PRIORITY.

saying, "I will put my Spirit upon him, and he will proclaim justice to the Gentiles" (Matthew 12:18). One of the by-products of concerning ourselves with justice is that it leads us towards closer union and communion with Jesus.

Matthew recalls the prophecy of Isaiah concerning the Messiah who will proclaim justice to the nations (Matthew 12:18). Furthermore, Deuteronomy 16:20 tells us that we are to pursue justice, and Amos 5:24 declares, "Let justice roll down like waters."

Repeatedly, four groups are singled out as special recipients of justice and mercy: the poor, the widow, the orphan, and the ostracized or alienated. We therefore ask God to give us a vision in which justice springs forth and injustices come undone. Because this is when the victim of trafficking is freed, the homeless are fed, and inequality is eradicated. We need to have the courage to stand up for truth—despite the opposition which might come about as a result. We must be the voices for the marginalized and the broken. Rather than being part of the prevailing ethos and ideologies or being part of the majority, we are called to believe in a cause that's worth fighting for.

This is what Joseph of Arimathea did. Joseph, like the heroes of faith before him, stood up for justice in the face of oppression and corruption. He followed in the footsteps of Moses, who stood up against Pharaoh. He followed the example of Daniel, who refused to adopt the mindset and customs of the Babylonian culture he was in. Joseph emulated the courage of Esther, who boldly spoke truth in the face of injustice and saved an entire people group. These battles for justice were deep within the Jewish heritage in which Joseph was living.

I think back to when I was a student in South Africa. We lived under apartheid, a brutal regime that believed its policies were sanctified by a biblical understanding, but it was so erroneous it hardly needs discussing. I remember the burning injustice that I felt as a student, and a white, privileged student at that. I tried to disagree both with the prevailing philosophy and the consequential actions being taken which required white and black people to be separate in schools and all public institutions. I spoke up against the injustice, and eventually, I became a chairman of the academic freedom committee at a university. There, we reaffirmed year after year that the university was a place where people could come together without regard to race, religion, or gender, even though this freedom was not, in fact, legal.

I recently returned to visit the university, and it happened to be graduation day. I was totally choked up to see a throng of students of every race and culture in their academic regalia and their proud parents on the steps of the Great Hall. It was deeply moving and could never legally have happened when I was there as a student. Tiny hopes haltingly expressed against the prevailing powers decades ago had become reality.

I believe there is within each one of us a passion to do the right thing. "The right thing" is not simply what best suits us at the moment; it is not governed by fleeting feelings. It is a passion for justice which is fueled by truth, anger, and courage. It is this same passion for justice written in the pages of the Bible. This passion for justice is born out of an understanding that God is just and that we are reflecting His desire for people to be treated with dignity every single day.

> THIS PASSION FOR JUSTICE IS BORN OUT OF AN UNDERSTANDING THAT GOD IS JUST AND THAT WE ARE REFLECTING HIS DESIRE FOR PEOPLE TO BE TREATED WITH DIGNITY EVERY SINGLE DAY.

I think of Nelson Mandela, the anti-apartheid revolutionary. He passionately fought for justice and stood up for what he believed was right, even at the cost of twenty-six years in prison.

I think of Winston Churchill. It was Churchill who stood against the prevailing view of the time that appeasing Hitler was the easiest way ahead. He was a lone voice. But he saved a nation, if not civilization itself. His suggestion that we should not ever underestimate the power of a dedicated minority is all the more trenchant because he lived it out in his own life.

I think of Rosa Parks, the woman who quietly refused to give up her seat for a white passenger on a segregated bus, thereby launching the Civil Rights Movement.

I think of William Wilberforce, a man who remains an example of what it means to be a truly courageous leader. He faced adversity head-on and never wavered in his resolve to abolish slavery and bring about the emancipation of those that were oppressed. He was both passionate about accomplishing his life's goal and unrelenting in his quest for bringing about meaningful and lasting change during a dark and difficult time in history. He committed his life to a higher calling: the pursuit of ending the British slave trade. He stayed in Parliament, going against the prevailing worldview, so he could advocate for the abolition of the slave trade.

We see examples of people standing up for justice on a daily basis. I think of the Occupy Movement in London. Some years ago, the Occupy Movement, a group of young people determined to see the reimagination of the market economy which had been tarnished by the great financial crisis, gathered in protest in London. Hundreds of them took over the steps of St. Paul's Cathedral, pitched tents, and refused to move. The City fathers were in a quandary and wished to have them evacuated and driven off the territory. The Cathedral authorities were trying to accommodate the expression of these ideals but were eventually forced to close the Cathedral. There was outrage on all sides —those who believed that the Cathedral should have been kept open as a place of sanctuary and those that believed that the protestors should have been hosed off the territory with high-powered water hoses. I felt very strongly myself that capitalism had indeed come adrift from its moorings— both in ethics and in values. The demonstrators were trying to highlight an injustice which required an urgent response if justice was to prevail.

The Bishop of London invited me to intervene and to try and bring about a peaceful solution, which seemed a daunting task, as there had already been violent clashes with the police. Through active engagement, with the demonstrators and with leaders of the City, further violence was averted. The demonstrators, having made their points, moved on with the assurance that the messages had been heard. Following the sit-in, we initiated a series of dialogues to raise awareness of these issues and to engage with those protesting, with consultations held at the very Cathedral from which the protestors had been barred.

There are many of these situations in which it is right to speak as a voice for the minority. We do so, not in order to be difficult or contrary to other opinions or prove some moral superiority, but rather because it is the great call of God to remain engaged with the key issues of society. Because wherever justice prevails, freedom

> **WHEREVER JUSTICE PREVAILS, FREEDOM FOLLOWS, AND THE KINGDOM ADVANCES. WHEREVER JUSTICE IS DENIED, FREEDOM FAILS.**

follows, and the Kingdom advances. Wherever justice is denied, freedom fails. The broader perspective gives us the confidence to speak on issues of justice even when it is a minority view. And that perspective comes from the Spirit of God, who enlightens the Scripture to us and reveals the heart of God. We need to be the ones in our time to speak, as Joseph of Arimathea did in his, against the prevailing ethos of popular opinion. The passion for freedom and the passion for justice run closely together; in order to be free, we must be just. We must be principled people, quick to obey God's truths. Joseph of Arimathea broke out of the council's parochial paradigm. He could see a much bigger picture. In this person of Jesus, there was the Messiah.

The calling of Joseph to stand up for justice is the same call to us. When a culture does not wish to be held accountable, then we need to speak truth to power—with courage, empowered by the Spirit of God, emboldened by the memory of Joseph. Sometimes, we are called to restate the principles upon which we believe a free society can live. To rebuke authorities whenever justice is denied. It is a calling that is inextricably bound up in the life of every ordinary Christian.

Joseph of Arimathea and all the aforementioned examples serve as signposts for us to follow in the same direction. They all had the courage to be sure about their purpose and values— not to let current circumstances dictate the future and to take decisive and intentional action. They all persevered in the midst of adversity and hardship and stood up for what they believed in. I believe this should inspire us to be optimistic in pursuing God's heart for justice. We can follow Joseph's example.

The night Jesus was arrested, he was brought before the chief priests, the officers, and the elders. He said to them, "This is your hour—when darkness reigns" (Luke 22:53, NIV). And indeed, darkness reigned from that moment on. Through the trial, through the crucifixion, through the death of Jesus, through the silence which followed.

Joseph, alone after the council meeting where he defended Jesus' innocence, forever surrendered the title of admirer of Jesus and exchanged it for the title of follower. Though he spoke against the injustice of killing an innocent man, he was overruled. He watched, heartbroken, as they crucified the person he believed was the Messiah.

06

UNDER PRESSURE

Joseph of Arimathea . . . took courage and went to Pilate and asked for the body of Jesus.
- Mark 15:43

I have been in very tense situations, both personally and professionally, where a decision had to be made, and the wrong decision came about in the end. That's when the horrible truth dawns that you could have done better. Sometimes emotions run high, and logic and reason become of secondary importance. That's when the video replay takes place. *What more should I have said? Could I have handled it better? Did I do everything I could have done?*

Joseph must have carried that weight with him as he watched the horror of Jesus being murdered. His heart must have been broken when he looked up at the dying Jesus on the cross. He must have felt burdened by the same thoughts that we are so often burdened by: *What more should I have said? Could I have handled it better? Did I do everything I could have done?*

His instinct would have told him he needed to negotiate something, to do something more. *How could he honor this man the way He deserved to be honored?* Wishing he could have done more to stop this, he must have thought about what he could do now. How could he help this man whom he had come to know and love? How could he honor Him? He had money and resources. He could provide an honorable burial after this unjust, dishonorable death. He must have thought about how his unique position granted him access to the Roman authorities. Unlike most, he could get an appointment with Pilate. His head must have calculated whether it was worth potentially sacrificing his position, his prominence, his prosperity to self-identify with an insurrectionist. But was that even his place? He was a secret disciple, not an obvious disciple. He wasn't known like Peter, James, and John. Surely they were more entitled to mourn and honor Jesus' death. Or what about Jesus' family? Joseph must have felt the pressure building, and yet, as we discover, he was prepared to work through this pressure.

Pressure draws out the conflict within us, and we become stressed and fearful when we're unable to see a way in which a decision will be made. We're forced to make a choice when we would prefer to duck. Here was Joseph waiting for the Kingdom of God—the long-held expectation of the way in which God would be moving—and at the same time privately harboring a real sense that Jesus was that promised Messiah. It must have been a growing inner conviction that led him to speak up before the council, and now that same inner conviction was telling him to do more, to speak up again and ask Pilate for the body. He would have been torn between the stress of the responsibility he felt and the fear that it wasn't his role to ask for the body.

That is often the case when we think that others have the responsibility to speak up or to take action. We think there are others more equipped and in better standing who are better able than we are to fix what is broken. *There are others.* But this is where things go wrong. We need to learn from Joseph that there are times when it is right to act, irrespective of whether others have a better standing and more responsibility to act.

We all face the pressure of making difficult decisions. Pressure builds when the stress of responsibility and the fear of the unknown infiltrate our decision-making process. Pressure is inevitable because we face decisions, fear, and stress every day. We can't control the fact that pressure is all around us, but we can control how we respond to pressure.

According to recent studies, one in four individuals suffers from stress.[10] This is the highest it's been since World War II. Concerns and anxieties rule our thoughts and actions. Uncertainty governs our minds like a thick black cloud that never seems to disappear. Potential for misfortune keeps us up at night. We worry about our economic climate with mounting bills,

> WE CAN'T CONTROL THE FACT THAT PRESSURE IS ALL AROUND US, BUT WE CAN CONTROL HOW WE RESPOND TO PRESSURE.

mouths to feed, families to provide for. We also have to deal with the dynamics of the press and social media, which can create an unusual dissonance within us. It means that we are always "on." While modern communication has increased the ease of our life, it has also significantly increased the speed at which it moves. Technology has advanced to such a degree that we have no frame of reference for how we should handle the sheer volume of data that is coming at us. Close-knit communities have given way to 24/7 connectivity, and surface-level swiping and scrolling has led to stress-induced living. Exchanges that once took weeks by mail can now happen on the other side of the world in seconds or minutes. This can lead us to do more and to be *expected* to do more. The pressure to respond quickly dominates our psyche and is now woven throughout the fabric of our culture and work environments.

Sometimes the pressure comes in small waves, testing us in little ways we can easily overcome.

At other times, it comes at us like a raging torrent that leaves us gasping for air. What-ifs and if-onlys collide to create a storm of stress and fear. It's as if a stampede of pressure is knocking at our doors every single morning, lurking to see whether we will cope with the day's demands.

As you're reading this chapter, I'm sure your mind goes back to a time or season in which you were thrown off course by daily demands. Within the space of twenty-four hours, you've ridden the rollercoaster of joy and celebration to fear and despair. Perhaps as a Christian, you've silently whispered and wondered if God can relate to what you are going through in your office, in your team, or in your home. Maybe you feel convicted to share your faith in your office, but you worry that it isn't your place. Maybe you feel you ought to help someone out financially, but you are worried that they will be offended. Maybe you want to take a stand against an injustice, but you are afraid you will lose your standing in the community.

Like Joseph, we too have decisions that need to be made and problems we need to resolve. We face the problem of holding together seemingly opposite desires; we want what is best and safest for us, but we also want what is best for others. In business, that's the conflict between the desire to maximize profit and the understanding of whether that is good for all the stakeholders. I've found in situations like this it is best to hold together the tension, but to be clear on what that tension is and to work through the issues both prayerfully but also importantly analytically. But also, it is important to talk through the conflicting thoughts with others so that you can arrive at a consensus or at least some degree of clarity. I find it helpful to name the issue, clarify the pros and cons of the problem, press the envelope, and test the assumptions on my own and with others. Then, and only then, act.

I know how difficult it can be to have so many people wanting different things from you. I know how it feels to receive one call with other people waiting impatiently on other phone lines. I even know what it's like to see a line begin to form outside my office door, with each person wanting answers to different, specific requests. Perhaps you planned a quiet night in to rest and instead, the doorbell rings suddenly. Perhaps you sought to empty your inbox at the office and instead bumped into a troubled colleague who needed some advice. Perhaps you wanted to get away for the weekend, but your team has let you down and the project in question isn't finished.

Jesus is well aware of how you feel (Hebrews 2:18). His heart has grieved. His plans have been squashed. His expectations have led to disappointment. He has faced pressure. Jesus can relate to the hassles, the headaches, and the heartbreak we can often feel in our lives. We are not alone in these feelings. Jesus experienced them too and set the perfect example for how to respond. Jesus modeled unity with God in the midst of pressure and fear; He showed us what unconditional trust in a perfect God looks like. God's call to trust Him is not a call to naïveté or ignorance. We aren't to be oblivious to the overwhelming stresses and pressures that life brings. We are to counterbalance them with remembering God's faithfulness: "We must pay much closer attention to what we have heard, lest we drift away from it" (Hebrews 2:1). God has hung His credentials in creation. He has referenced His faithfulness in Scripture, and He is the commander of every stress, every fear, and all the pressure we will ever face. He can be trusted and provides us with the power to face the pressures of our everyday lives.

> JESUS CAN RELATE TO THE HASSLES, THE HEADACHES, AND THE HEARTBREAK WE CAN OFTEN FEEL IN OUR LIVES.

Joseph of Arimathea speaks to this reality. He acted not out of fear, but out of trust in God.

As Christians in the world, we risk persecution. We must prepare for it and we are to resist it when it comes. Today more than 200 million Christians in sixty countries experience imprisonment, torture, and death for their faith.[11] Such statistics have a way of silencing us. We can be numb to the reality of such persecution. The statistics are more than academic. In whatever form, whether physical or verbal, persecution will come to us if we profess faith in Jesus Christ.

The spiritual oppression which Christians face in the marketplace is real. We might not all be facing guns and swords from terrorist attacks, but we do deal with critics and accusers. We face the academics and the educated who call our faith primitive and insist that it is no longer relevant to our culture. In the workplace, board members can pressure you to compromise your values or integrity. Whenever you have weak moments, co-workers are there to make it their goal to call out your hypocrisy and dub you as a fake.

Some of us have experienced family members who have put pressure on us to adhere to traditional customs. Friends have mocked our faith and belittled our convictions. If you're a student in college, professors and contemporaries perhaps laugh at your beliefs and worldview. You face the daily pressure to conform to people's ideals and to forsake your convictions. Persecution will

> PERSECUTION WILL COME. THAT'S SOMETHING WE CAN BE SURE OF. BUT HOW MANY OF US ARE PREPARED TO DEAL WITH IT, AND THEN BE ABLE TO RESIST IT?

come. That's something we can be sure of. But how many of us are prepared to deal with it, and then be able to resist it?

I think of the persecution that the early church suffered as the gospel was spreading and the Spirit was moving after Jesus' resurrection. In the first few chapters of Acts, we see that the fruit of the disciples' ministry and obedience was evident to all—all except the religious rulers of their day. The religious rulers sought to silence the disciples by pressuring, threatening, and persecuting them.

For some time following Jesus' resurrection, the early church enjoyed low-hanging fruit and great testimonies of God's faithfulness. The ripple effect of Pentecost brought in over 3,000 lost souls. The church was healing the sick, preaching the word, and praying together in homes. Their practical demonstration authenticated their proclaimed declarations. The church grew at a rapid rate. Their social media accounts would have been booming. They would have been tagged in photograph after photograph. Hashtags of baptism and deliverance would hit our feeds. The momentum was with the early church. That describes the first three chapters of the book of Acts. But then the tone shifts. A page is turned. Acts 4 begins to unfold.

The Church is barely out of its embryonic stage and in walks the persecution: "The priests and the captain of the temple and the Sadducees came upon them" (Acts 4:1). Peter and John must have been thinking of the crucifixion. The cross. The nails. The crown of thorns. It was all coming back to them.

During Jesus' last days on earth, Peter had nothing but a bad record when it came to the pressure of persecution. He floundered under pressure in the garden of Gethsemane, as he drew his sword to protect Jesus and cut off the right ear of the soldier (John 18:10). Then when Jesus was arrested shortly after, Peter denied that he knew Jesus to three different people, seeking to distance himself from persecution. When pressure came, Peter did not respond well.

So far, the persecution was getting to Peter. Yet, post-resurrection, as the church was being built, something shifted: the empowering spirit came upon them. Every test had been a failure up to that point, but this time, Peter decided to stand firm. Even if he was shaking in fear, he stood tall, boldly proclaiming Jesus as Lord. Peter boldly affirms in verse 12 that "there is salvation in no one else, for there is no other name under heaven given among men by which we must be saved" (Acts 4:12).

What was the reason for Peter's change of heart? I think it was the same reason Joseph of Arimathea moved from being a secret disciple in the shadows to embracing Christ publicly as his Lord. An inner conviction, born of the Holy Spirit, who reminded them of all Jesus did for them—an inner voice that told them to take heart.

Peter had been with Jesus. He had encountered Jesus face to face. Peter experienced forgiveness and restoration on the beaches of Galilee, when he saw Jesus post-resurrection and he ate with Him. And because of what Peter and the other disciples had witnessed and whom they encountered, silence and submission were no longer an option: "We cannot but speak of what we have seen and heard" (Acts 4:20).

When I read this account of Peter, it makes me want the same level of courage and boldness. But being so bold and courageous means also being mocked, scorned, and criticized. When we take a stand for Christ, people will misunderstand us. We must expect to be marginalized. But when we experience the risen Christ, He empowers us to stand firm when the pressure of persecution comes. When we experience that pressure, we must be like Joseph and Peter and bolster courage to act, in spite of the fear and stress we face.

Courage grows as we spend time with Christ. This is what the disciples experienced. If we want to have courage to stand against the pressures of misunderstanding tomorrow, then we need to spend time in God's presence today. It is then that people will realize that we, like Peter and Joseph, have been with Jesus. And

> **WHEN WE TAKE A STAND FOR CHRIST, PEOPLE WILL MISUNDERSTAND US.**

they will make a choice as to how they respond. Jesus doesn't want us alarmed when pressure comes. He wants us to be prepared.

As Joseph steps out of the shadows and embraces what will surely result in intense pressure to toe the line, he steadies himself, sets his face like flint. An appointment with Pilate awaits.

07

BUSINESS HEAD

*Joseph . . . asked Pilate that he might take
away the body of Jesus, and Pilate
gave him permission.*
- John 19:38

Where were the disciples now? In the wake of Jesus' death, where were Jesus' friends who had observed His every move, who had listened to His every word? They had entered the Holy Week with Jesus, watching Him laugh as children sang, watching Him weep as Jerusalem ignored Him. Watching His silence as priests accused Him. Watching in despair as Pilate turned on Him. They had seen Jesus' power: blind eyes opened, fruitless trees withering under the sound of His voice. Money changers vacating the temple as He turned tables, Lazarus' tomb opening. They'd heard His promises. They heeded His warnings. Despite everything that they saw and everything that they'd witnessed, now they were nowhere to be seen.

We could be forgiven for thinking it was a mistake to choose these uneducated, inexperienced, and now unfaithful men who didn't step up when Jesus needed them. Surely the next person God would use to undertake such an important task—requesting the body of Jesus and asking to bury it—would be a charismatic and larger-than-life leader of leaders.

What we read and discover in the Scriptures, however, is quite different. God instead uses an individual, a secret disciple, who steps up after Christ's death. Joseph didn't have an intricately planned strategy to implement, nor a big team to execute it. It was not his function to bury the body— that would have been the family—but he took the first step. He took the initiative and the first part of the initiative was to acquire permission to access the body.

> GOD INSTEAD USES AN INDIVIDUAL, A SECRET DISCIPLE, WHO STEPS UP AFTER CHRIST'S DEATH.

I can only imagine the state of his heart as he plucked up his courage and went boldly to Pilate. He had been opposed to the decision of the council, and therefore the decision of Pilate, to have Jesus executed on a cross. Who would have really cared if he had simply taken the body of a convicted criminal without asking? Arguably no one. Then he wouldn't risk tarnishing his reputation.

But Joseph was a respecter of authority and understood that sometimes one has to follow bureaucratic procedures in order to achieve objectives. He knew that action was required, but he also respected the process and channels through which those actions had to flow. He wanted to act honorably, and he knew he had to act fast.

For a start, there was the logistical issue. Numbers of crucified bodies would be stacked in a heap to be buried or burned, depending upon whether family members claimed them. Where was Jesus' body? Had it been separated from the crowd? Could Jesus be identified amidst the stack of dead bodies? At this point we can only speculate. But we do know from historical sources what the four possible outcomes for Jesus' body were:

1. Jesus' body would be left exposed as carrion to be consumed and decompose in public.
2. The Roman soldiers would take the body down and put it in a communal burial plot.
3. Members of the Sanhedrin would come, under obligation, and perform a ritual dishonorable internment.
4. Relatives of Jesus might plead for the body to be released to them for burial.

Joseph would have to do the latter in place of Jesus' relatives by going boldly to Pilate, making sure he had a legitimate and plausible plan as to what to do with the body. A great amount of courage was needed to self-identify with a person who Pilate had just condemned to death. There is an argument that it was not Pilate's decision to give the rights to Jesus' body—that the body belonged to the family. But one has to bear in mind the gruesome facts of the case: This was a condemned criminal. This crime of causing insurrection against the Romans meant that His life was in the hands of the Roman governor. Pilate had the power to burn and dispose of the body. Burying Jesus wasn't a given.

As the scene unfolds, we observe how Joseph goes to Pilate. Pilate probably gave him the audience, given the prominent person Joseph was in the community. This is another good example of the way in which he would steward his influence effectively. There was no guarantee, of course, that Pilate would release the body. But Joseph, knowing this, went to Pilate to ask for the body of Jesus. Pilate called the guards to find out whether it is true that Jesus has died. I can just imagine the scene. Pilate surely asked Joseph, "Why on earth do you want the body? You have no familial link." What can Joseph say? After all, he is not asking for the bodies of the two thieves crucified with Jesus.

Eventually, after Pilate had received word that Jesus was indeed dead, Pilate gave Joseph the body.

That's when Joseph swung into action. Joseph was a practitioner. He understood the Jewish customs. Joseph knew that certain processes had to be fulfilled and specific procedures had to be followed. He drew upon his resources and brought Nicodemus alongside him. Nicodemus brought the spices and linens. John states that Nicodemus brought seventy-five pounds of myrrh and aloes (John 19:39). Together, the two men found, claimed, and carried Jesus' body to the tomb. They struggled with the dead weight of His body and the weight of the spices. Using these spices for the burial of a criminal would have been inconceivable; spices were usually reserved for the royal and the wealthy. A very heavy load of aromatic scent was lugged through town to settle around the broken body of an executed man—an extravagant outpouring. They must have had large households and servants, but they did not send others to do this job for them. Two wealthy Jewish men, who did not even dare to proclaim openly their adoration of the living Jesus, were now blatantly grieving in the wake of His death.

They also made themselves unclean by touching the body shortly before the Sabbath, in light of the Old Testament law that says, "Whoever touches the dead body of any person shall be unclean seven days" (Numbers 19:11). With seventy-five pounds of sweet-smelling spices, Joseph and Nicodemus, in that defeated and crushing hour, stepped up to the plate. They anointed Jesus' body for burial. They bound Him up. They found the tomb—Joseph's tomb—an unused tomb. They placed Him in the tomb, rolled the heavy stone across, and, to their knowledge, said goodbye to their friend forever.

Of course, with thousands of years between the event and where we are now, we can easily over-spiritualize it. Not everything is religious inspiration. There are times when perspiration, planning, and following processes are as integral to achieving overall objectives as if it were some prophetic moment. Neither the prophetic nor the pragmatic have primacy in the Kingdom of God. Joseph of Arimathea knew there was a preparation day. He knew the Sabbath was coming. He knew that certain actions needed to be taken. He was, therefore, fully absorbed in the planning of his actions. To me, this is an extraordinary encouragement. I have always lived by the Augustinian sentiment and mantra, "Pray as though evereything depended on God. Work as though everything depended on you." God's purposes require our participation. God will often not do what we can do for ourselves. Therefore, the work I do is not in vain, but my careful planning, and the time I put into strategizing, is not wasted as I utilize the gifts God has given me.

I have often been struck by the way in which religious conversation can be so easily trapped in the metaphysical, causing the physical to be forgotten. It seems a common mistake for believers to substitute pragmatism and practicality for "thoughts and prayers." Of course, I believe there is a time for prayer and seeking God. In fact, the highest call of the Church is the call to prayer. If we as a Church succeed at everything but fail at prayer, we've failed. I also believe when we make prayer our strategy, every other strategy begins to succeed. However, we cannot use praying on our knees as an excuse for not participating with our hands. Faith in action involves both.

> WE CANNOT USE PRAYING ON OUR KNEES AS AN EXCUSE FOR NOT PARTICIPATING WITH OUR HANDS. FAITH IN ACTION INVOLVES BOTH.

It was two business people who were there when the practical stuff had to be done. They got their hands dirty and became unclean in order to show respect to the one they put their hope in. Joseph and Nicodemus show us that it isn't good enough merely to be followers of Jesus Christ; we must also get our hands dirty doing the work that He calls us to.

I have learned over the years that people watch the way I act more than they listen to what I have to say. My identity as a follower of Christ has been seen in the way I have conducted myself in practical settings: from the boardroom to the team meeting to the way I speak to my colleagues. It's in our practical acts that people can read and see Jesus. For many people, they will read our lives before they ever read Matthew, Mark, Luke, or John. The Apostle Paul says that we are a "letter of recommendation . . . to be known and read by all" (2 Corinthians 3:2). For many people, it will take a practical demonstration of love before they get a revelation of love.

To call ourselves children of God is one thing, but to be called a child of God by those who watch our lives is another thing altogether. Like Joseph, we must have courage and take action. Being a disciple is not just thoughts and prayers. It is doing hard work with our hands; it is showing love and devotion through our actions. Without a demonstration, my declarations about following Christ are empty. Paul says we are the "aroma of Christ" (2 Corinthians 2:15). We are to act like Christians in all our interactions and transactions as Christ leads us throughout the day. This is where we will carry the aroma of Christ. Are we prepared to act in a way that displays that we are followers of Jesus? We must ask ourselves the question: where are our spices? Have we ever experienced that moment, when the exorbitant price of following Christ becomes insignificant and we can't help but work to usher in the Kingdom of God?

Sunday's dawn hadn't crept over the horizon yet. All the disciples saw was darkness, but unbeknown to them, the dawn was winning already. Reconciliation and redemption were already streaming through the night as two leaders settled the cloths around Jesus' broken body, practically attending to the needs of their crucified Messiah.

08

JOSEPH AND NICODEMUS

He was accompanied by Nicodemus.
- John 19:39, NIV

When Joseph took action and responsibility for the body of Christ, he did not act alone. He had help and support from Nicodemus. They were colleagues, and perhaps friends, but what bound them together now was the undeniable effect that Jesus had had upon both of their lives.

After seeking permission for Jesus' body and it being granted from Pilate, Joseph enlisted another secret disciple to help him perform the burial rituals. I can imagine the scene that followed. The body that encased a Messiah was lifted and laid in the arms of

Joseph of Arimathea and Nicodemus. "He's yours," said the soldier indignantly. "Take him away!" These two wealthy men were not accustomed to this type of activity. Yet their hands moved quickly to their task, both acutely aware that they couldn't do this without the other. I picture Joseph of Arimathea kneeling down behind the lifeless, drooped head of Jesus. Perhaps he was holding back tears or wiping the blood-stained contours of Jesus' face. I imagine Nicodemus taking out a cloth that was wrapped and tied around his belt and passing it to Joseph, inviting him to clean the blood that came from the lashings, the beatings, the crown of thorns.

In this moment, the two Jewish leaders and members of the ruling council look at one another with mutual understanding. This is the last procession. They lift the lifeless body of Jesus and set it on the linen. Parts of the body are now anointed and perfumed with seventy-five pounds worth of spices. As Nicodemus anoints the body of his friend with aloes and myrrh, he must have been containing his emotion. He must have thought back to the night he went to Jesus. He was scared then, and he must have been scared now, as he looked nostalgically at the young rabbi. The hierarchical society of Jerusalem wasn't going to look kindly on two of their esteemed religious leaders burying an insurrectionist. After the interplay between Nicodemus and the religious leaders in John chapter 7, the consequences of their so called "rebellion" would no doubt have repercussions to both their job and their status in the council. But, for Joseph and Nicodemus, the choice was obvious. They risked losing their status, yes, but gained the privilege of burying their Savior.

To me, this is so intriguing. What bound Nicodemus and Joseph together? They formed a partnership. Was it the partnership of disappointed disciples? Perhaps the shame they both carried from their lack of open witness to Jesus? Was it that disappointment of unmet expectations of the coming Messiah that joined them together in their grief?

My mind lingers on the scene. This body of Christ was now in their hands. The person whose miracle-working, powerful preaching, and mesmeric personality had captivated the attention of everyone He encountered.

John records that "the tomb was close at hand, [and] they laid Jesus there" (John 19:42). The two of them, perhaps one cradling his head and one holding his legs, carried the broken body. Wounds in His hands and feet. His side impaled by a soldier's spear. His head punctured by the crown of thorns. His back raw from the lashings He received. Joseph and Nicodemus cleaned up the blood, anointed the broken body, then they laid His crumpled form in the tomb.

> FROM BEGINNING TO END, THEIR PARTNERSHIP CAN SERVE AS A SIGNAL TO US THAT THE BODY OF CHRIST IS BEST SERVED WHEN WE DO SO TOGETHER.

There is extraordinary power in the imagery of these two prominent men honoring the life of Jesus together. Not only did they help each other carry the weight of the body of Christ, they also helped each other carry the grief they both experienced. Joseph knew he couldn't do it on his own. He knew he needed help, and he asked for it. From beginning to end, their partnership can serve as a signal to us that the body of Christ is best served when we do so together.

For Christians, here is a lesson that we should learn. It is one that I'm particularly excited by as I look to the millennial generation—the sharing and caring generation. We need thriving communities to fulfill our God-given purpose. I see this generation of millennials teaching lessons which, I hope, will leave a lasting mark on generations to come. There is a greater spirit of working together, joining together, partnering, and co-operation than I have ever seen before.

Over the course of my years in finance, I've seen many joint ventures. Many partnerships, many

> **WE NEED THRIVING COMMUNITIES TO FULFILL OUR GOD-GIVEN PURPOSE.**

cooperative activities, and endeavors. Some succeed and some fail. I've also seen the consequences when individuals wish to be sole entrepreneurs and fail because of their unwillingness to join with others. When we join with others, we have support for when we go through tough times; we have people to help us carry the load when life becomes overwhelming, and people to celebrate with when life is full and joyous.

There is something compelling about a partnership which is not simply functional. Yes, we're each doing a different piece and fulfilling a purpose. We play a functional role in our daily lives and in our churches. *We need the software engineer and the software writer. We need the pastor, the worship leader, the volunteers.* There is definitely a functional element to community, but it doesn't stop there. As we look at Joseph and Nicodemus's case, we see a deep relational link. A link that enables them to work together towards a common purpose. Amidst all that had gone on in Jerusalem in that fateful week, they were able to share their disappointments and hopes, their fears and grief.

Life has a way of driving us into hiding and isolation. We think that we should be self-sufficient, but comfort comes through fellowship and community. God distributes pieces of His eternal jigsaw puzzle to all manner of people. When we share, hang out, confess, and pray, we become the Body of Christ. When we partake in community, we are built up in our faith and in our lives. It is through partnership that we flourish. Paul said, "The church is his body; it is made full and complete by Christ, who fills all things everywhere with himself" (Ephesians 1:23, NLT). As Ann Voskamp writes, "Growing in grace is corporate; we are a body and the body of Christ needs to be informed and reformed by the other parts."[12] This is a much-needed message in our day and age when we have the possibility of going throughout the whole day without speaking to anyone. In order to experience the fullness of Christ and His grace and His hope, join in partnership and in community with other believers.

> IN ORDER TO EXPERIENCE THE FULLNESS OF CHRIST AND HIS GRACE AND HIS HOPE, JOIN IN PARTNERSHIP AND IN COMMUNITY WITH OTHER BELIEVERS.

Our culture is set up for individualism and isolation. We wear AirPods to the gym, we communicate via WhatsApp and text message. We put on our noise cancelling earphones just to get a break from the sheer volume of information being thrown at us on a daily basis. It's the only way we can cope with the exposure we experience. But something powerful happens when we enter into partnership with others that will never happen in isolation. In isolation you see your reflection, but in partnership you see yourself and the world through the eyes of others. Partnership expands your perspective while helping you achieve your goals faster. Only in community can we work towards one common goal and fight for what we believe in with like-minded people.

> **NONE OF US CAN DO WHAT ALL OF US CAN DO.**

None of us can do what all of us can do. We can't get away from this as we read Jesus' commission to the disciples: "You will be my witnesses" (Acts 1:8). Jesus wasn't speaking to one individual here; when He said *you,* He meant *all of you, together.* He didn't issue individual assignments. He didn't move one-by-one down the line and crown each individual:

You, Peter, will be my witness . . .
You, Andrew, will be my witness . . .
You, James, will be my witness . . .
But rather: "The sum of you will be my witnesses."

Jesus works in partnership. He modeled partnership to his disciples, and after Jesus' death and resurrection, they followed in His footsteps. For that reason there are no singular pronouns in the earliest description of the Church:

And they devoted themselves to the apostles' teaching and the fellowship, to the breaking of bread and the prayers. And awe came upon every soul, and many wonders and signs were being done through the apostles. And all who believed were together and had all things in common. And they were selling their possessions and belongings and distributing the proceeds to all, as any had need. And day by day, attending the temple together and breaking bread in their homes, they received their food with glad and generous hearts.
- Acts 2:42-46

The passage contains only plural nouns and pronouns: "They devoted themselves," "All who believed," "They were selling their possessions." No "I" or "my." They were in this together, as partners. We as Christians are in this together. We are more than followers of Christ "because we are members of his body" (Ephesians 5:30). We, *together*, are His Body, and because of this, we work together. The hand cannot discount the foot. The head cannot act in opposition to the knees. The eyes must not refuse to partner with the feet.

Now if the foot should say, "Because I am not a hand, I do not belong to the body," it would not for that reason stop being part of the body. And if the ear should say, "Because I am not an eye, I do not belong to the body," it would not for that reason stop being part of the body. If the whole body were an eye, where would the sense of hearing be? If the whole body were an ear, where would the sense of smell be? But in fact God has placed the parts in the body, every one of them, just as he wanted them to be.
- 1 Corinthians 12:15-18

This passage shows us that we are intimately, intricately, and intentionally connected. We cannot build the Kingdom of God or fulfill our purpose on our own.

Paul later goes on to say, "Make every effort to keep the unity of the Spirit through the bond of peace" (Ephesians 4:3, NIV). Unity and interconnectedness matter to God. What if the missing ingredient for changing the world is partnership? When believers agree, Jesus takes notice. He shows up. "When two of you get together on anything at all on earth and make a prayer of it, my Father in heaven goes into action. And when two or three of you are together because of me, you can be sure that I'll be there" (Matthew 18:19-20, MSG). This is an astounding promise. God hears our prayers and puts us to work, but we must work together. We can't divide around doctrine or separate because of stylistic preferences. We won't accomplish anything. When workers split, the Kingdom doesn't advance.

> UNITY AND INTERCONNECTEDNESS MATTER TO GOD. WHAT IF THE MISSING INGREDIENT FOR CHANGING THE WORLD IS PARTNERSHIP?

The early Church found a way of partnering with one another. They found common ground in the death, burial, and resurrection of Christ. Because of this commonality, they built community and lives were changed. They helped each other out in terms of doctrine and practice (Acts 8:14-25). They relocated leaders to strengthen other situations (Acts 11:19-23). They sent individuals and teams on short-term strengthening visits (2 Timothy 1:18). They sent money to help each other and bless the wider society

(Acts 11:28-30). And they helped advance the gospel together and plant churches (Romans 15:24). Isn't this how God works? The Church is a microcosm of God's plan. She is the bride of Christ, and one day Jesus will come back for her. This body is made up of many parts. No one person can do everything, but everyone can do something. And when we do, statements such as these will be said about us: "The apostles testified powerfully to the resurrection of the Lord Jesus, and God's great blessing was upon them all. There were no needy people among them" (Acts 4:33-34, NLT).

God did not call us to live and work in isolation, but placed us in the body of Christ. A body that works at its best alongside every other believer in Jesus throughout the world, in every age. Let us grow as a team, work as a team, and live as a team in partnership. Our only hope is to work together. And if all of us work together, there is hope.

I am often struck by the number of Christian organizations who could work even better if they were to work together. The true and successful partnerships are the ones where there is a common ethos and a collective purpose which binds together the groups *relationally*. People coming together and interacting relationally—irrespective of their backgrounds and work—with Jesus as the center of their focus and activity results in successful partnership. When we focus on our commonalities and build relationships on the foundation of what we have in common, then we will experience growth and true community.

Partnership is an often overlooked, yet vitally important, aspect of New Testament Christianity. Although the ministry of

Paul and other prominent New Testament leaders was in some ways unique (and therefore in some ways unrepeatable), the pattern of partnership is duplicatable. God still provides suitably gifted people to facilitate such partnerships today. Paul used the word "partnership" to describe both church leaders and churches working together: "As for Titus, he is my partner and fellow worker for your benefit" (2 Corinthians 8:23). "I thank my God in all my remembrance of you . . . because of your partnership in the gospel" (Philippians 1:3-5).

Partnerships are necessary for mission, maturity, and momentum. Our mission from Jesus is to take the gospel to our communities and the nations, to both Jerusalem and to the ends of the earth (Matthew 28:19). How could any of us do that alone? But if we can organize ourselves properly and relationally around a common purpose, we can contribute meaningfully to the mission.

We all have different things we can contribute to the overall mission. Whether it's financially or prayerfully, our time or our energy, together our mission can be healthier, stronger, and more sustainable. In terms of maturity, we will not reach our full maturity in Christ without outside perspective and input. Joseph and Nicodemus teamed up together, because partnership provides support and synergy. Whether it is creating internal partnerships between colleagues or departments or larger partnerships between businesses, harnessing

WE NEED TO FIND NEW WAYS TO DRIVE COLLABORATIVE INNOVATION, BOUND TOGETHER BY THE HOLY SPIRIT WITH THE COMMON GOAL OF GLORIFYING JESUS.

the strengths and abilities of others from different corners of your specific ecosystem is one of the most strategic ways for businesses to scale innovation and solve complex challenges. In today's fast-paced environment, a do-it-alone approach is not the best strategy for momentum. It is the same in our spiritual lives. We need to find new ways to drive collaborative innovation, bound together by the Holy Spirit with the common goal of glorifying Jesus. Partnership matters.

As Joseph and Nicodemus climbed the outcrop of Golgotha, as they stared at one another and strategized about who would do what, never could they have imagined the power that would come from the tomb in which they placed the dead body of Jesus. Their obedience and interaction with one another set the stage for the greatest miracle ever known.

09

SILENT SATURDAY

He rolled a big stone in front of the entrance to
the tomb and went away.
- Matthew 27:60, NIV

To fulfill the preparation requirements before the Sabbath sunset on Friday, Joseph takes Jesus' body in his hands and, in the final act, puts it into his tomb. There is no hint here of the new life that is about to spring into the world and utterly change the course of history. He rolls a stone across the entry, shutting Jesus off from the whole of creation, from all the people. The women who were watching at a distance recognized the finality of this act, lamenting their failed hopes, expectations, longings, activities, and ministries. Hoping for these to be germinated with power from on high, only to realize that a stone has been rolled across the entrance.

There is a divine pause. The feverish activity of the week has gone. This is the end. This is silent Saturday.

But Joseph did not see the divine pause. What he saw was the pointlessness.

It takes deep meditation to step into the mind and the heart of this man. A dejected leader. His messianic hopes for the Kingdom of God dashed. His expectation that Jesus would be the Messiah destroyed. In the depths of disappointment, he performed, perhaps mechanically, the ritual tasks of honoring the body of someone who he had hoped would be the liberator of Israel. Joseph had hoped, together with so many others, that Jesus would be the final revelation of the Messiah. And now he grieves as he holds in his arms the lifeless, blood-spoiled body. The pointlessness of the whole exercise must have overwhelmed him.

As we think of him, perhaps we allow our minds to stray to the people on the way to Emmaus with that haunting remark born out of the depths of their hopelessness: "But we had hoped that he was the one to redeem Israel" (Luke 24:21). They had given up their livelihoods to follow this rabbi. A great teacher, for sure—but the Messiah? Yet place after place, teaching after teaching, miracle after miracle, Jesus had won their hearts and corrected their doubts. They had followed Him all the way to Gethsemane, and now they groaned with confusion as they tried to piece together the traumatic events of the final week.

John paints the scene for us and tells us, "It was still dark" (John 20:1). Dark as the sun dipped behind the horizon. Dark with the atrocities that had unfolded that harrowing Friday afternoon.

Dark with the disciples' betrayal. The only degree of light that shines out of the darkness is Joseph of Arimathea. One of the last to acknowledge Jesus during his life. The first to hold Jesus after His death. The last one to see Him as he placed Him in the tomb.

The traditional burial spot of the empty tomb requires us to use our imagination. Over two thousand years ago, it was Joseph's tomb. Now it's a garden tomb or a high-domed cathedral covered with opulent decor and paintings. A sepulcher marks the spot where Joseph lay Jesus. Forty-three different lamps hang high above the tomb and a candelabra is positioned just in front of it. Made with solid marble and cornered with exquisite architecture. It's hard to view it and see what would have been its original state and to imagine the surroundings.

However, one thing that can be seen as you peer through the rock-hewn tomb of Joseph is this: it was dark. It was dusty. It looked uncared for and unkept. Joseph's tomb for Jesus would have been tiny, with low ceilings, forcing someone of average height to squat. Joseph could have put Jesus in a dark, poorly-lit, compact room and sealed the door. The irony, that the light of the world was shut in a tomb. Nothing is more hopeless or dark than a grave. Nothing is so dormant as a tomb.

We have the benefit of Church history and the Scriptures to show us what happened on Sunday. However, Joseph didn't have the privilege of knowing what Sunday had in store. Joseph was not expecting the world to change forever. For him, his hope was gone. The man who spoke words of life and forgiveness had been silenced. The hands that healed blind eyes were now pierced.

The hopes of a liberating Messiah: *dead.*
The expectation of miracles: *dead.*
The man of action: *dead.*
The teacher: *dead.*
The wise rabbi: *dead.*
The encourager of this new Kingdom: *dead.*
The authoritative master of the scriptures: *dead.*

On this silent Saturday, Joseph was not only grieving Jesus as a beloved leader, but he was also grieving his loss of faith. Though he surely was experiencing disappointment, confusion, and grief, I wonder if there was still a spark of hope inside him? In the silence of that Saturday, I wonder if there was just a hint from within Joseph of Arimathea that perhaps this really was the Messiah?

We don't know a lot about this day. We have no passage to read, no knowledge or wisdom to share. All we know is this: Saturday was silent. The day between the struggle and the solution, the question and the answer. The Passover activities had ceased and the Sabbath had begun. It was dark. Everyone was still. And God seemed silent.

Saturday's silence torments us. Why the heartache of the pointlessness of life? Why did God not move swiftly to raise Him from the dead? Why the wait? Is God angry? Did I disappoint Him? God knows your career is hanging by a thread, your finances are in the pit, your marriage is a mess. Why doesn't He act? What are you supposed to do until He does? There are times in the life of every Christian when it appears that we carry the dead weight of our unrealized expectations, our unanswered prayers. When we experience God's silence in our lives, in our homes, in our churches, in our cities and countries, there is no flicker of hope as we nurse the disappointment. It is this silent Saturday that becomes the hallmark of the true Christian disciple.

These are the emotions that Joseph would have felt. He waited. In silence. Jesus told them He would return. But did they really think Jesus would? Everything that Joseph had placed his hope in was buried in that rock-solid tomb. He must have mourned and imagined how he would live his life without Jesus in it. He must have felt regret and remorse about not stepping out in his association with Jesus sooner. Was this really it? What if Jesus didn't come back? What if hope stayed buried? As Joseph carried the lifeless weight of Jesus to the grave, Joseph's body ached all the more for a breath to come from Jesus' lungs and His presence to come to life. To walk with Him. To learn from Him. To be with Him.

AND YET, THROUGH THIS LONGING, WE LEARN SOMETHING. WE ARE ALWAYS WITH HIM.

And yet, through this longing, we learn something. We are always with Him. In this in-between stage—in the liminality, the gap, those moments in life when God seems silent—we are silent *with* Him. It is an act of faith to believe that He speaks even when we don't hear Him. That He is there even when we don't see Him. That He is alive, even when He appears to be dead. That it is the beginning even though it looks like the end.

In John 12, Jesus reminds us that a grain of wheat needs to

fall to the ground and die before new life can come. There is that moment in which the new seed has to crack through the ground— the darkness before the light appears. These are the moments of high testing. It's those who come through these dark times who become the true leaders. There is an unimaginable depth of spirituality that occurs when your journal recording God's activity in your life is blank. Do you have faith when the silence of Saturday comes?

We have to face the utter desolation of the silent Saturday. I do not know of any Christian leader who hasn't been to that place. If this is you, take courage and see in Joseph an example. What do you do in the silence? You remember what God has done in your life and you listen, because in the silence God still speaks. Our pain is not pointless. We lack the perspective to see how parts of our lives fit into God's overall plan. Cancer, disabilities, accidents, suffering, and other sorrows and deep disappointments with how life turns out appear devastatingly pointless. However, just because we don't see any point in suffering doesn't prove there is no point to what we are facing.

> **WHAT DO YOU DO IN THE SILENCE? YOU REMEMBER WHAT GOD HAS DONE IN YOUR LIFE AND YOU LISTEN, BECAUSE IN THE SILENCE GOD STILL SPEAKS.**

Recently I attended the farewell concert of Paul Simon in Hyde Park in London. Sixty-one thousand people were jammed in the park. As the light began to fade over the buildings and darkness started spreading, the single guitar solo pierced the darkness as

Paul Simon sang the haunting lyrics of "The Sound of Silence." I observed the crowd, young and old, every generation mesmerized by both the melody and the lyrics by the memories of their own times of silence.

Silence does have a sound. It can sound like the grueling moments of loneliness, despair, or waiting, but it can also sound like the most profound song in the world, resonating with depth and intensity. Because, even in the silence, when it appears that there is no God activity, it's an interlude—a time when He draws us closer to Himself. Even in the silence, there is the sound of the gathering promise that He will speak. In those times of silence, when everything seems pointless and when there appears to be no purpose to my pain, I have discovered that there are several things we can do.

Firstly, in the silence and in the midst of what appears to be a pointless time of life, do not worry. You are not alone. God is in control. Pain of uncertainty and anxiety, which accompanies major shifts in our lives, can be so overwhelming and can shake us in our calling. In these times, we need to remember four words: *God is with us.* This is the declaration—"Immanuel, God with us" (Matthew 1:23)—which marks the beginning of Jesus' life.

And the end of His life is marked by Him saying, "I am with you always, to the end of the age" (Matthew 28:20). He knows and He cares. He is preparing. He may be silent, but He is not absent.

Secondly, don't waste the pain. When things don't go according to your plan, when you are disappointed, when you are grieving, don't let your passions, your desires, your gifts, your relationships with others and God wilt and waste. It's time to stop sitting and start searching, stop wasting and start working. This time is the crucial training, mentally, physically, spiritually, and emotionally, for what is ahead. Trust that God is good and has a plan. Waiting on Him to speak new life into this season does not mean pausing or halting your purpose in any way. There's purpose in the silence.

Waiting in seasons of silence is a spiritual workshop. Look at the Technicolor dream boy Joseph, of the Old Testament, thrust into a "silent Saturday" in the bowels of an Egyptian prison. He was not idle though. No, he had the opportunity to exercise his gift of prophecy, which two years later resulted in his release from his very demanding period of waiting and his promotion to prime minister of Egypt.

Likewise, Joshua was required to march seven times around Jericho before taking the city (Joshua 6). Our work of preparation may be of a spiritual or practical nature—it tends to be a mixture of both. But there is always plenty we can do as we wait.

Thirdly, don't waiver. Silent Saturdays can turn your mind to begin to wander away to sinful thoughts. Don't let distractions, doubts, and questions destroy your destiny. Instead, do as David did in the Psalms, where he tells us that "I waited patiently for the Lord" (Psalm 40:1). Waiting is a part of the spiritual discipline essential to everyone who is following Jesus. But then, significantly, the psalmist

> WAITING ON HIM TO SPEAK NEW LIFE INTO THIS SEASON DOES NOT MEAN PAUSING OR HALTING YOUR PURPOSE IN ANY WAY. THERE'S PURPOSE IN THE SILENCE.

added, "He inclined to me and heard my cry." I have found the first part—waiting—almost unbearable at times. Yet when I have clung to that second half of the promise, I have not been disappointed.

Finally, don't be weary. Easier said than done, of course. But it begins with an attitude shift. Look at Abraham (twenty-five years of waiting), Moses (forty years of waiting) and Jesus (thirty years of waiting). They all received a call from God and had to spend years in obscurity as God cultivated their character and competencies before elevating them to a place of influence. Sometimes the task for which we are being prepared has not yet been fully disclosed to us. And the more demanding the new calling, the tougher the preparation might be. You are in good company in the waiting.

I have often reminded myself of the story of the persistent widow who relentlessly pursued the judge for the outcome she dreamed of, until he finally granted the request (Luke 18:1-8). She had no standing before such a prominent man, but day in and day out, she was persistent in her requests. She might not always have felt like turning up before the judge; however, her request was worth remaining resilient in the midst of consistent rejection. This story inspires us to labor in prayer to see our dreams fulfilled. I believe that each silent Saturday we encounter is developing our faithfulness. As we trust God in these seasons of grief and silence, we reflect on His faithfulness.

The Scripture says that God is always at work, for the good of everyone who loves Him (Romans 8:28). This is His character. He loves you too much not to work for you. He's busy. He's active.

He's doing what is right in the right time. I just invite you to believe this, to trust that everything is going to work out in the right way, according to His schedule and not yours. In trusting Him and waiting on Him, you will hear Him speak in the silence. You can trust Him. As with Christ, you can endure the silence of Saturday. Be patient. His inactivity is not apathy. It is in the silence that Christ speaks, and Christ will show Himself strong. Jesus will not leave us in our silent Saturdays. He decides when it's time to end the silence. He decides when our Sunday comes. He speaks to us in His timing, and His timing is always perfect.

Exhausted from grief, Joseph lies down on Saturday and finds sleep quickly. As he sleeps, the darkness passes. Dawn is breaking.

10

THE PEOPLE OF THE SMALL PRINT

He is not here, for he has risen, as he said.
Come, see the place where he lay.
- Matthew 28:6

The time following Jesus' death was shrouded in silence and darkness. Laying palm branches at the feet of Jesus must have felt like a distant memory. The triumphant entry had been eroded by tragedy. Hosanna gave way to helpless despair.

Was there any purpose in Joseph's actions? Claiming Jesus' body from Pilate—what was the purpose in that? Carrying His dead body from the pile of crucified victims in Golgotha—what was the purpose in that? Devoting his own tomb as the space where Jesus could be put to rest. Why? Joseph acted in spite of how he must have felt. And he decided that, though it was over, there was still a purpose to it all. It's hard to be optimistic when you have witnessed that kind of finality. In that moment, the prophetic words of Jesus littered throughout the Scripture would be hard for him to recall. Little did Joseph know that, in the spiritual realm, the darkness and pain of Friday were to give way to the light of Sunday morning.

Joseph wasn't to know with any certainty that his deeds would be depicted in the Scripture for generations to come. Yet he faithfully did what he could do with what he had. This is no easy thing. At times, our purpose can feel doubtful and we call into question why we do what we do. This must have been how it felt for Joseph. We can't ignore the hours that we hear nothing about. Living in the tension of waiting, grieving, and suffering. His hopes entombed in the sealed grave where his friend and master lay. Did he trust God when the pain seemed pointless? Did he believe God could weave the fragmented, broken story together? His words and actions indicate an affirmative *yes*.

> LITTLE DID JOSEPH KNOW THAT, IN THE SPIRITUAL REALM, THE DARKNESS AND PAIN OF FRIDAY WERE TO GIVE WAY TO THE LIGHT OF SUNDAY MORNING.

So often, we are clueless as to how our purpose fits into anything of greater significance. I'm sure Joseph must have replayed the events of the last few days over and over again. Thinking to himself: *What now?*

I imagine Joseph going to the tomb on Sunday to pay respects to a man that had forever changed his life and his purpose. As he nears the tomb, he is reminded of the events of Friday. He winces, viscerally affected by the memories of carrying the weight of Jesus' lifeless body. But as Joseph gets closer, he sees that the heavy stone he used to seal the tomb is rolled away. He runs to it as his mind races to try to figure out what has happened: *Did someone steal His body? Wasn't someone supposed to be guarding it?* He runs to find the disciples and as he does, he is told the good news: Jesus is alive! Many witnesses testify. *Could it be?* Joseph is filled with hope and joy—elated by the image of his empty tomb. Restoration. Rebuilding. Renewal of all things. A new starting point in history. Hosanna restored.

Death was defeated. New life had begun. Pessimism gave way to optimism. But not a faint optimism. A sure and certain hope grounded in the reality that Jesus had risen. Death was done. Desolation and destruction would not have the final say.

I can imagine Joseph's pace increasing, as he ran to his own tomb. Could he dare to believe that the rumors were true? When he saw the first sign of resurrection—an empty slab, abandoned burial cloth, a folded linen shroud—no doubt he ran in to examine the tomb like Peter did, as described in John's Gospel.

Joseph gets his tomb back. Just as Jesus said He would: "Destroy this temple, and in three days I will raise it up" (John 2:19). During Jesus' life, Joseph was a weak believer, a secret disciple, unsure. But, in that moment, when he saw the empty tomb, he must have known the purpose of it all. When Jesus was raised to life, purposelessness died in the grave of Jesus.

You say the pain and waiting feels pointless. With Christ, there is purpose. You say the storm is too much. It is temporary, and Christ is with you. You say the thorn is too painful. His grace is sufficient. You say the cross is too heavy to bear. Jesus has carried it first.

When the silent, doubt-filled Saturdays leave you feeling purposeless, you can turn to Christ for help. This is what the resurrection infuses into our daily lives. Hope, new life, restoration, redemption, fulfillment. Even on the dark Saturdays, we have what Joseph never had: the assurance that there is life. This scene should comfort and encourage us. The next time you find yourself in despair, remember what Joseph must have witnessed. When you're entombed by fear and doubt, remember what Joseph must have observed. The next time pain and pointlessness attack and attempt to push you into the darkened tomb, remember what Joseph must have seen. The tomb was empty. This is the Christian hope, and this Christian hope is verified by the miracle that left Joseph's tomb.

YOU SAY THE CROSS IS TOO HEAVY TO BEAR. JESUS HAS CARRIED IT FIRST.

We can now build our lives on the promises of God. We now have purpose. Nothing is pointless. Even the most devastating situations can be turned around by God's grace and resurrection power. A word that's unbreakable, a victory of such finality. We stand on this unshakeable and precious promise of God. Death has been swallowed up in victory. It's a promise that's more precious than anything else we could ever grip or hold onto.

Joseph of Arimathea was a wise man. He did his duty, fulfilled his purpose, and became an example for generations of Christians. We now have hope in what he witnessed: that Jesus Christ rose from the dead. The underwriting of the new life, the new historic moment on the cross. We now live among the sunlit fruits of life. The stone that he placed across his own tomb, subsequently sealed by imperial command, was rolled away. What was dead became alive. What was broken became whole.

The historic hopes of Israel were vindicated. Jesus rose as the Messiah even after He died a miserable traitors' death at the hands of the authorities. In this moment, the Messiah and the Kingdom of God that Joseph had longed for became vindicated in the person of Jesus.

A day before he saw the long-awaited Messiah *dead*.
The vindication of Israel: *dead*.
The hope of salvation: *dead*.

But everything changed that Sunday morning.

The hopes of Israel: *alive*.
The prophetic expectation: *alive*.
The King of Kings: *alive*.
The hope of humanity: *alive*.
The same power that resurrected Jesus from the dead: a*live and active within us.*

His resurrection proved that He was, and is, the Son of

God. And so, if Joseph was there as one of the disciples, he would see that the miracles were alive. The hopes alive—the expectation, the aspiration, the prophetic insight alive. The future of redeemed mankind alive.

Now, by His Spirit, we are able to live in this new aliveness. We are energized to share this good news with others. It fuels us every day, in every sphere we find ourselves influencing and participating in. If the resurrection didn't happen, it'd be pointless. Joseph's work would have been in vain (1 Corinthians 15:12-19). But the resurrection power living within us sustains us and helps us to not be separatists waiting for heaven when we die, but a chosen people, engaging with humanity and offering hope through the power of the Holy Spirit.

Joseph prepared us to know that we must live by faith, acknowledging that Jesus has consummated His Kingdom, while still aching for that fulfillment to come about. God has given us His Spirit to remind us of all the things Jesus has said, so that we can keep our peace and hold onto our joy amidst the challenges and vicissitudes of life. There are times when we need to claim the resurrection power in our lives, even when we cannot see it and even when there are dead ends to our endeavors. So we cry, *Hallelujah, Jesus Christ is risen from the dead!* That is the power that transforms our day-to-day lives. The privilege of knowing that Jesus Christ transforms and makes all things new.

> NOW, BY HIS SPIRIT, WE ARE ABLE TO LIVE IN THIS NEW ALIVENESS. WE ARE ENERGIZED TO SHARE THIS GOOD NEWS WITH OTHERS.

And so we now have a new tension. The acceptance of silent Saturday, but with the Spirit of God proleptically acting to remind us that there is a Sunday. That there is a future. That there is a resurrection. In that respect, we are never utterly defeated or downhearted. Painful as those interim days are, we are able to see the powerful, unrestricted, enabling force of the one who overcame death. Because of that triumphant Sunday, we all now have access to the resurrection power that raised Christ from the grave. The resurrection power that can mend relationships, the resurrection power that can heal wounds, the resurrection power that can help us overcome all trials. All we have to do is look to the one who overcame the

> PAINFUL AS THOSE INTERIM DAYS ARE, WE ARE ABLE TO SEE THE POWERFUL, UNRESTRICTED, ENABLING FORCE OF THE ONE WHO OVERCAME DEATH.

powers of darkness, made a spectacle of the forces of evil, and sits enthroned at the right hand of the Father. The King of Kings reigns with the Spirit of God forever and ever. Energizing us, mobilizing us, driving us to see His Kingdom established. In the life of every citizen in the community, in every city, in the Church, and in our country.

Low self-esteem can wrap us back in grave clothes, keeping us from walking out our purpose. Self-belief can rob us of the resurrection life we now have. But when our lives feel purposeless, we look at the empty grave and remember that death is not a dead end. We can step away from the very things that entomb us. We can exit the tomb, realizing that the light of the world has pierced the darkness, and we are equipped to accomplish everything we've been assigned to complete. We can take this resurrection light to our families and friends, to our workplaces, in our alone time. There is no aspect of our lives that the resurrection light cannot reach.

I am often asked, "How is it possible to be a Christian in the workplace? How have you sustained forty years in investment banking?" My response is always geared to viewing life in light of the resurrection. It is certainly not easy to find an empty tomb in the midst of our busy, everyday, fast-paced lives. The pressures and demands from people are always vying for our attention. The speed of information is constantly downloading to our phones and filling our heads and hearts. So, you may have to take some time out to meditate on it and see what Joseph saw. You may, like Joseph, have to see it for yourself. See the vindication of the resurrection and the implications it has to our purpose here on earth. Run your fingers through the empty sheets of linen folded in a corner, once used to hold Jesus' body. Smell the spices that anointed it, accentuating the fact that the stench of death will not prevail.

> WE CAN TAKE THIS RESURRECTION LIGHT TO OUR FAMILIES AND FRIENDS, TO OUR WORKPLACES, IN OUR ALONE TIME. THERE IS NO ASPECT OF OUR LIVES THAT THE RESURRECTION LIGHT CANNOT REACH.

But we don't stop there. And while the future life awaits us, there is work to be done and there is purpose to be fulfilled. We are to get on with our work, knowing that it will not go to waste.

At the centerpiece of God's renewed creation we will discover that everything done in the present world in the power of the Holy Spirit will be confidently declared, included, celebrated, and completely transformed for God's glory.

How can you usher in the signs of hope that the resurrection has now been established? Every life has purpose. There is an aliveness to the pragmatic, daily demands that life puts before us, and we can fulfill those responsibilities either consumed by our own darkness or enlivened by the light of the resurrection.

Resurrection light is not just for the people who get all the air time. It's not just for the Peters and the Pauls. It's for the hidden figures, the people of the small print, those who feel marginalized as if they are but footnotes to the story of others. Those who, like Joseph, now perceive the world as God intended it to be—redeemed. They have a perspective that reveals their new position in Christ. They see broken things with the potential to be restored.

> RESURRECTION LIGHT IS NOT JUST FOR THE PEOPLE WHO GET ALL THE AIR TIME. IT'S NOT JUST FOR THE PETERS AND THE PAULS. IT'S FOR THE HIDDEN FIGURES, THE PEOPLE OF THE SMALL PRINT . . .

They can see the potential for stagnation and decay to be healed. The power of the Spirit energizes us to engage with such phenomena and to bring change and transformation to our communities.

With a resurrection perspective, we do not shy away from culture and we do not remain in our silos, so preoccupied with an individualistic spirituality that we don't engage or create restoration. In a world that is fueled by modern technology and the arts, we embrace, share, and champion the resurrection light; we must demonstrate the power of the gospel and use the resources available to us to see new communities of life come into being. Because creativity is a distinct characteristic of resurrection. It's as if God has brought out a blank canvas to be drawn on with His power. We are to co-create this new world which points towards the ultimate resurrection of our earthly bodies and the day when the New Earth will be restored in all things. Creativity is the essence of new life, new beginnings. Art can be a reflection of our deepest human stories, celebrating everyone's stories and purpose, celebrating the people of the small print.

We may be people of the small print, but our lives have significance because they are infused with the very energy of God, with the light of the resurrection. The same power that raised Jesus is available to you and me (Romans 8:11). The question is: do we have eyes to see how empowered we are? The resurrection of Jesus is like an exploding flare that announces to Christian believers: "You have purpose!" After all, Joseph's story is not just to tell us what Jesus did. It's to tell us what Jesus still does today. Which brings us to the final easel that stands before us. It has on it a nearly blank canvas. A few marks from left to right. But there are plenty more brushstrokes to be painted. That painting belongs to you.

God, by His Spirit, wants to pick up the brush and paint your life with purpose. You've seen how Joseph stepped out, how he made his life count and how he made up for lost time. As we pick up our Bibles and stand in front of the gospel writers' accounts of Joseph of Arimathea, it provokes us to stare at our own canvases and determine what portrait we are working with God to paint. Embrace your purpose, fueled by the power of the Holy Spirit. Whether you leave a legacy through education, innovation in technology, your impact as a business person—no matter what your occupation, you have purpose, and God is using your position to bring resurrection light to those around you. Whatever you put your hand to, use your passion, gifts, and talents to pursue purpose in light of the resurrection.

As we portray what Jesus has done for us, we will be able to release His resurrection power within us. People of the small print, faithfully carrying out courageous endeavors for the cause of Christ their King. In Joseph, we see ourselves in an extraordinary calling of an ordinary man.

Joseph of Arimathea is a blueprint for us to follow. When Jesus died, Joseph had choices. He could have joined the Zealots, those who sought to rebel against the Roman Empire. A driven and courageous man would fit in well with those seeking to start a revolution. He could have given up and withdrawn from society like the Essenes, those who

> WHATEVER YOU PUT YOUR HAND TO, USE YOUR PASSION, GIFTS, AND TALENTS TO PURSUE PURPOSE IN LIGHT OF THE RESURRECTION.

congregated in communes devoted to a life of poverty and austerity. Living a quiet, safe life with like-minded individuals. Maybe some would have followed him. He could have gone back to the Sanhedrin court and gone on with his life. He did none of these things. He went to Pilate and asked for the body of a seemingly rebellious prophet and rabbi, because Joseph found purpose in Jesus. His prominence and position no longer mattered to him in light of Jesus' death. His position was already in tatters. The price he paid was nothing compared to what he saw on the cross. He found his life by losing it. He looked at the cross, and he saw an unfinished story; he looked at the empty tomb and saw a masterpiece that needed to be framed. The canvas upon which Joseph's life has been painted records an ordinary life lived with extraordinary impact. The portrait of Joseph spurs us on to live with purpose in the present and change the future we are all moving towards.

Some of us will have platforms, the majority of us won't, but we all have influence. And we will all be famous in heaven as Christ says to us, "Well done, good and faithful servant" (Matthew 25:23). And somewhere in the great gallery of heaven, your canvas will stand as a testimony to the empty tomb. Perhaps it will be positioned next to the portrait of perseverance depicting Joseph of the Old Testament. Or it might be next to the portrait of faithfulness depicting Joseph the earthly father of Jesus in the New Testament. But, more than likely, it will be next to Joseph of Arimathea, with just a few verses attributed to him in Scripture, but a life fulfilled, a legacy left, a purpose completed, a faithful servant rewarded. A person of the small print, whose life points towards the throne seated high above

> **THE CANVAS UPON WHICH JOSEPH'S LIFE HAS BEEN PAINTED RECORDS AN ORDINARY LIFE LIVED WITH EXTRAORDINARY IMPACT.**

every other canvas. The centerpiece of the gallery. The portrait that depicts purpose fulfilled, power established, and pain eliminated forevermore. That's a promise worth standing on. That's a promise worth living for. The Holy Spirit is alive and active within us, ready to invade the places and spaces we inhabit on a daily basis. In our families, in our homes, in our churches. There is a picture in each of us ready to be painted upon the canvas of creation. We are invited to participate in the restoration and renewal of all things, if we would just say yes, and allow God to choose the paint and colors He wishes to display through us.

There is an allotted space with your name on it. When I was re-awakened to the prophetic word I had received at the conference in London over twenty years ago, I was reinvigorated and re-inspired to see that prophetic vision become a living reality in my own life. I want to live out that prophetic vision and equip a generation: "You're here to be

> REMEMBER THE EMPTY TOMB AND RELEASE YOUR STORY INTO THE WORLD.

light, bringing out the God-colors in the world" (Matthew 5:14, MSG). By the leading of the Spirit, our canvases can be filled with colleagues, friends, and loved ones who encounter the resurrected Jesus in their everyday lives because they came into contact with us. Our brush can be surrendered to the Artist's hand and the Artist's purpose for the canvas upon which He will paint.

What will your canvas depict? In case you're ever in doubt, look to Joseph of Arimathea's portrait. Then look up at the throne. Remember the empty tomb and release your story into the world.

ACKNOWLEDGMENTS

I particularly want to thank all those who have, somewhat to my surprise, taken seriously the possibility of writing a book on Joseph of Arimathea, about whom we know so little. In particular, I am extremely grateful to Esther Fedorkevich and her team, Lauren Hall, Whitney Gossett, Jill Welborn, and Tori Thacher, who have been both an encouragement and critic of the book.

Rob Wall has patiently worked through editing the manuscript with me, and I am very grateful both for his insight and for his ability to keep me to a manageable timetable within the hectic schedules of the day job.

Above all, I would like to acknowledge all those who will read this book and who feel that their contribution is not enough— who feel their work in the Kingdom is but the small print, even a postscript to the stories that are written by more famous or more prominent people. Joseph has been an encouragement to me and I hope Joseph will be an encouragement to you. I want to acknowledge your contribution however small you might think it to be in contributing to the growth of the Kingdom. It's ordinary people, in ordinary daily activities, who can do extraordinary work in the kingdom.

Thank you to Israel Fouche for his support and insight throughout the writing process. I would also like to thank Georgina and Nick Philps and my wife, Fiona, for reading the manuscript and for their warmly critical comments.

Thank you to Nicky Gumbel, Vicar of HTB, and for HTB Church for their encouraging response when I tested this message, "The Cross of Courage," on Joseph of Arimathea—it was the spark that encouraged me to start work on the manuscript.

In passing, it's worth acknowledging the almost total absence on any search engine on a full-length message of Joseph of Arimathea. To all those pastors who have missed this great man of the small print, I look forward to hearing many a message preached on Joseph in the years to come!

ENDNOTES

1. "In His Iconic Portrait, Winston Churchill Is Scowling Over a Lost Cigar." PetaPixel. March 08, 2013. Accessed July 08, 2019. https://petapixel. com/2013/03/08/in-his-iconic-portrait-winston-churchill-is-scowling-over-a-lost-cigar/.

2. Young, Bruce. "Meaning of "The Face of the Other"." Meaning of "The Face of the Other". January 01, 1970. Accessed July 08, 2019. https:// faceofother.blogspot.com/2007/03/meaning-of-face-of-other.html.

3. Avary, Myrta Lockett. *Virginia Girl in the Civil War.* D. Appleton and Company, 1903.

4. "The Messiah We Hope For." RZIM. Accessed July 08, 2019. https://www. rzim.org/read/a-slice-of-infinity/the-messiah-we-hope-for.

5. "Qavah - Old Testament Hebrew Lexicon - New American Standard." Bible Study Tools. Accessed July 08, 2019. https://www.biblestudytools. com/lexicons/hebrew/nas/qavah.html.

6. "Prosdechomai - New Testament Greek Lexicon - New American Standard." Bible Study Tools. Accessed July 08, 2019. https://www.biblestudytools. com/lexicons/greek/nas/prosdechomai.html.

7. Quote attributed to Edmund Burke (in a letter addressed to Thomas Mercer).

8. As quoted in *Spirituality and Liberation: Overcoming the Great Fallacy* (1988) by Robert McAfee Brown, p. 136.

9. Kierkegaard, Soren. *Bread and Wine: Readings for Lent and Easter.* Maryknoll, NY: Orbis Books, 2005. 55-60.

10. Osdjay. "Work Related Stress Is at Record Levels." TUC. May 15, 2018. Accessed July 08, 2019. https://www.tuc.org.uk/northern/blogs/work-related-stress-record-levels.

11. Miles, Jennifer. "Christian Persecution May/Jun 2018." Israel My Glory. Accessed July 08, 2019. https://israelmyglory.org/article/christian-persecution-may-jun-2018/.

12. Stetzer, Ed. "One-on-One with Ann Voskamp on Going to Back to School at the Wheaton College Grad School." The Exchange | A Blog by Ed Stetzer. Accessed July 08, 2019. https://www.christianitytoday.com/edstetzer/2019/february/one-on-one-with-ann-voskamp-on-attending-wheaton-graduate-s.html.

NOTES

NOTES

NOTES

NOTES

NOTES

NOTES

NOTES

NOTES

NOTES

NOTES